THE

OLD TESTAMENT

WISDOM LITERATURE

JOB, PROVERBS, ECCLESIASTES, SONG OF SOLOMON

by

JOHN T. WILLIS

Published By
BIBLICAL RESEARCH PRESS
1334 Ruswood
Abilene, Texas
79601

THE
OLD TESTAMENT
WISDOM LITERATURE

by JOHN T. WILLIS

◆

Copyright © 1982
Biblical Research Press

◆

Library of Congress Catalog Card No. 81-69494
ISBN 0-89112-145-5

◆

TABLE OF CONTENTS

PREFACE

The Wisdom Literature of the Old Testament supplies a great deal of teaching which modern man will find very up-to-date and practical. *Job* deals with the struggles of a man who is striving to serve God, but is suffering severely, for no apparent reason. *Proverbs* deals with a wide variety of subjects ranging from worship to God to the use of the tongue, usually in brief two-line maxims, but sometimes in rather lengthy poems like that on the good wife in chapter 31. *Ecclesiastes* emphasizes that all earthly pursuits are vanity when viewed from a purely human point of view for the purpose of pointing man to God. And *Song of Solomon* depicts the beauty of pure marital love.

One should study this booklet with several good modern English translations of the Bible at hand. Each passage cited should be studied with care. Other helps should be consulted, including Bible encyclopedias, commentaries, special studies, and journal articles (see the Bibliography at the end of this volume).

My wife, Evelyn, and I would like to dedicate this study to the following administrators at Abilene Christian University and their wives: Chancellor John C. Stevens and Ruth, President William J. Teague and Peggy, Vice-President for University Advancement Gary McCaleb and Sylvia, Former Assistant to the President Don Drennan and Rudith, Graduate Dean Floyd W. Dunn and Pauline, and University Dean Edward M. Brown and Edna; and to the Library Staff at Abilene Christian University, who have provided so much help during the past ten years of my stay at the University, particularly Director of the Libary Kenneth Roach and Anita, Callie Faye Milliken, and Delno Roberts.

Lesson I

THE ANCIENT WORLD OF WISDOM

"Incline your ear, and hear the words of the wise"
(Proverbs 22:17)

A reasonably large portion of the Old Testament belongs to a distinctive type of writing which has come to be called "Wisdom Literature." This includes the books of Job, Proverbs, and Ecclesiastes, but also possibly other portions of the Old Testament, or parts thereof, such as certain psalms (e.g., 1, 49, 73), the Joseph narrative in the book of Genesis (Genesis 37-50), verses here and there in the prophetic literature (e.g., Isaiah 28:23-29; Hosea 14:9), and the like; as well as extra-biblical literature including the Old Testament apocryphal books of Ecclesiasticus (Ben Sira, Sirach), Wisdom of Solomon, and the wisdom poem in Baruch 3:9-4:4, and works from other ancient Near Eastern countries such as Egypt, Assyria, and Babylon. Among the various groups of functionaries mentioned in the Old Testament and ancient Near Eastern literature are not only kings, judges, priests, and prophets, but also sages or wise men. It is generally agreed that it is they who were responsible for the wisdom literature.

The Wise Men

There are numerous references to Israelite wise men and wise women in the Old Testament. Wise men are among those in official circles in Jerusalem who plot to take Jeremiah's life (Jeremiah 18:18). Jeremiah condemns the wise men who shirk their divinely given responsibility to teach the people God's word in deference to lies

(Jeremiah 8:8). The Lord declares that the wisdom of Judah's "wise men" will perish because the Jews draw near to God with their mouth but not with their heart (Isaiah 29:14). The book of Proverbs states that the wise are responsible for many of the proverbs in this inspired Old Testament book (Proverbs 22:17; 24:23). Joab engages "the wise women of Tekoa" in southern Judah to take an imaginary court case to David in the hope of persuading him to restore absalom to his favor (II Samuel 14:1-24), and "a wise woman of Abel of Beth-maacah" saves her city from destruction of the hands of Joab by having Sheba beheaded and his head thrown over the wall (II Samuel 20:14-22). As is true with the prophets and priests of the Old Testament, some of the wise men were good and some were evil.

The Old Testament also frequently refers to groups of "wise men" and "wise women" in other nations. When Sisera, the Canaanite of Harosheth-ha-goiim and captain of the host of Jabin of Hazor, does not return from the battle against Israel as soon as normally expected, his mother and her "wisest ladies" conclude that he must be gathering an inordinate amount of spoil for them (Judges 5:29). Ezekiel declares that the prince of Tyre thinks he is "as wise as a god" and "wiser than Daniel" (Ezekiel 28:2-6), and Zechariah characterizes Tyre and Sidon as "very wise" (Zechariah 9:2). Obadiah (verse 8) refers to "the wise men" of Edom. Several Old Testament texts refer to "the wise men" of Babylon (cf. Jeremiah 50:35; Daniel 2:24, 27; 4:6; 5:8). King Ahasuerus of Persia consults his "wise men" to find out what should be done to Vashti for refusing to carry out his wishes (Esther 1:13). Joseph (Genesis 41:8, 39), Moses (Exodus 7:11), and Isaiah 19:11-13) face "the wise men" of Egypt. Both Agur (Proverbs 30:1) and Lemuel (Proverbs 31:1) are from Massa, which apparently is a region in North Arabia, and some of their "words" are preserved in the inspired book of Proverbs. The Bible states that "Solomon's wisdom surpassed the wisdom of all the people of the east, and all the wisdom of Egypt" (I Kings 4:30).

2

Thus the Old Testament makes it quite clear that all nations have their "wise" men and women.

Ancient Near Eastern Wisdom Literature

In light of these biblical references, it should not be surprising that a great deal of Wisdom Literature has been unearthed by archeologists in various parts of the ancient world. Most recently, in fact, the Ebla tablets, discovered at the modern site of Tell Mardikh in Syria, have revealed that this thriving ancient city of approximately 260,000 inhabitants had its own scribal school, in which scribes from various Mesopotamian cities came to learn and to share their wisdom. *Ancient Near Eastern Texts*, edited by J. B. Pritchard, and *Babylonian Wisdom Literature*, by W. G. Lambert, contain English translations of portions of several ancient wisdom writings, which the reader may wish to consult to get a flavor of the scope and nature of ancient Near Eastern Wisdom Literature.

Egypt

The biblical comment that "Solomon's wisdom surpassed all the wisdom of Egypt" (I Kings 4:30) assumes that the wisdom of Egypt was very famous by his day (ca. 961-922 B.C.). Several lengthy pieces of Egyptian wisdom literature are extant.

(1) *The Instruction of Ptah-hotep*, vizier of King Izezi of the Fifth Dynasty (ca. 2450 B.C.), contains numerous instructions to this vizier's son, several of which are very similar to maxims in the book of Proverbs. For example, he tells him: always be submissive in the presence of your superiors (cf. Proverbs 23:1-8); if you are entrusted with carrying a message, be reliable (cf. Proverbs 13:17; 25:13); never betray the friendship of an equal or an inferior (cf. Proverbs 25:9-12); love your own wife and be totally committed to her alone (cf. Proverbs 5:15-19).

(2) *The Instruction for King Meri-ka-re* by his father (end of the twenty-second century B.C.) admonishes very high ethical practices, as speaking justice in one's own house, not oppressing the widow, encouraging and helping the younger generation, and making no distinction between the rich and the poor.

(3) *The Instruction of Amen-em-het* (second quarter of the twentieth century B.C.) is that of a pharaoh directed to his son, Since he was overthrown by treachery within his own household, he admonishes his son to trust no one.

(4) *The Instruction of Ani* (a lesser official living toward the end of the Egyptian Empire) is an admonition to his son to refrain from talking a lot, to serve his god faithfully in external worship and inner life, and to marry young and be faithful to his wife. This piece of literature contains a strong admonition to avoid the prostitute, which is very similar in thought to Proverbs 6:23-35 and 7:6-23.

(5) *The Instruction of Amen-em-opet* (tenth to sixth centuries B.C.) consists of instructions by this Overseer of Grains to his courtiers as to how to get along in the society of their superiors and elders. It is divided into thirty chapters (cf. Proverbs 22:20), and contains numerous parallels to Proverbs 22:17-24:22. A few examples may be cited.

Sixth Chapter:
"Do not carry off the landmark at the boundaries
of the arable land, nor disturb the position
of the measuring-cord."

Proverbs 23:10:
"Do not remove an ancient landmark
or enter the fields of the fatherless."

Thirteenth Chapter:
"Better is praise as one who loves men
Than riches in a storehouse;

4

Better is bread, when the heart is happy,
Than riches with sorrow."

Proverbs 16:8:
"Better is a little with righteousness
than great revenues with injustice."

Sixteenth Chapter:
"Do not lean on the scales nor falsify the weights,
Nor damage the fractions of the measure."

Proverbs 20:23:
"Diverse weights are an abomination to the Lord,
and false scales are not good."

Twenty-First Chapter:
"Spread not thy words to the common people,
nor associate to thyself one (too) outgoing of heart.
Better is a man whose talk (remains) in his belly
Than one who speaks it out injuriously."

Proverbs 20:19:
"He who goes about gossiping reveals secrets:
therefore do not associate with one who speaks
foolishly."

(6) *The Onomasticon of Amen-em-ope* (ca. 1100 B.C.)
contains a list of some 600 things the Egyptian god Ptah
is said to have created, including creatures in heaven,
earth, and water. It calls to mind the biblical lists of
things created by Yahweh in passages like Job 38-39
and Psalms 8, 104, 147, and 148.

(7) *The Dispute over Suicide* (end of the third millennium B.C.) is a discussion between a man who is weary
of life and his soul. The man finds life unbearable and
so contemplates suicide, much like Job yearning for
death because his suffering is greater than he can bear
(Job 3). Like Job urging his friends not to let him down
in his hour of deep need (Job 6:14-30), he begs his soul
not to abandon him, and like Job pleading with God to
hear him (Job 6:8-10), he urges the gods to hear his

5

plight. Like Job (Job 9:15,20), he affirms his innocence and assures his soul that he will be highly respected among the deceased. At first, the man's soul urges him not to commit suicide, but to give his life over to pleasure; but later he promises to be faithful to the man whatever he decides to do.

(8) *The Protests of the Eloquent Peasant* (early twenty-first century B.C.) insists on the importance of justice being done to the poor. After a long discussion and series of legal actions between a peasant and a Chief Steward over the way the Chief Steward's vassal had treated the peasant, the Chief Steward finally rights the wrongs his vassal had done to the peasant.

Mesopotamia

There are also Mesopotamian texts which contain striking similarities to the Old Testament wisdom literature.

(1) *The Counsels of Wisdom* (probably fourteenth or thirteenth century B.C.) is a collection of moral exhortations perhaps by a vizier to his son. It consists of approximately 150 lines and admonishes such virtues as showing kindness to the poor, avoiding evil companions, returning good for evil, and not using bad language.

(2) *The Instructions of Suruppak* (ca. 2000 B.C.) consist of counsel of a king to his son Ziusudra, the Sumerian flood hero. Among other things, the king urges his son to submit to an old man's instructions and to avoid being alone with another man's wife.

(3) *I will praise the Lord of wisdom*, sometimes called *The Babylonian Job* (second half of the second millennium B.C.), is strikingly similar to the Old Testament book of Job in several ways. A noble named Shubshi-meshre-shakkan describes many calamities which struck him, including loss of wealth and health. He affirms that his suffering is undeserved, and concludes that man can-

not know why the gods do what they do. Marduk appears in a whirlwind and vindicates him, and he is restored to his former health and prosperity.

(4) *A Dialogue about Human Misery*, sometimes entitled *The Babylonian Theodicy* (ca. 1000 B.C.), relates a dialogue between a man and his friend consisting of 27 stanzas of eleven lines each. The initial speaker raises difficult questions, like Why do the gods not defend helpless orphan children? or Why should the firstborn son be favored above the other chidren of a family? or Why are criminals successful?, to which his friend patiently attempts answers, some of which seem satisfactory and some which do not. Finally the speaker concludes that men are evil because the gods made them that way.

(5) *A Pessimistic Dialogue between Master and Servant* relates a conversation between a master and his slave, in which the slave agrees with his master no matter what he says. The reason for this behavior is that the servant sees no meaning in life. Thus this piece is similar to the pessimistic outlook reflected in the book of Ecclesiastes.

The Wisdom of Ahikar

The famous *Story of Ahikar* has been preserved in Aramaic (fifth century B.C.) as well as in other ancient languages. Ahikar advises his nephew to discipline children for their own benefit (cf. Proverbs 23:13-14), guard his tongue, be wise in dealing with the king, and learn to keep secrets.

A comparison of Old Testament wisdom literature with that of the surrounding ancient world reveals at least three things. First, all men grapple with basically the same enigmas and problems of life. Second, the Old Testament writers sometimes borrowed from earlier ancient Near Eastern literature, just as the author of the book of Joshua borrowed from the now lost Book of Jashar (Joshua 10:13) or Paul from pagan poets (Acts

17:28; I Corinthians 15:33; Titus 1:12) or Jude from I Enoch (Jude 14-15). Of course, they did this under divine inspiration. And after all, a truth or historical fact need not be stated or written initially by an inspired speaker or writer to be correct. Third, all in all it is clear that Israelite wisdom literature is superior in its religious assumptions and teachings to the wisdom writings of Israel's neighbors.

Old Testament Apocrypha

The apocryphal books of the Old Testament contain some striking similarities with and contrasts to the canonical books recognized by Protestants.

canon = the books of the Bible officially recognized by the Church

small a. = any writings of questionable authorship or authenticity

(1) *Ecclesiasticus* (ca. 180 B.C.) is an attempt to defend Judaism from Hellenism by arguing that true wisdom is to be found in Israel. Much of the book contains proverbial material, although each proverb usually extends for several verses in contrast to the one verse maxims in the book of Proverbs. Chapter 24 identifies Wisdom with the Jewish Law, which is said to have existed before the creation of the world.

(2) *The Wisdom of Solomon* (first half of the first century B.C.) represents an attempt by an Alexandrian Jew to help preserve the ancient faith of his fellows by emphasizing that Judaism has true wisdom in contrast to all competing pagan philosophies. In 7:22-8:1 he gives a long list of the qualities of wisdom, which he identifies in this work with the Spirit of the Lord.

(3) The wisdom poem in *Baruch* 3:9-4:4 (perhaps first century A.D.) declares that true wisdom comes from God alone, and identifies wisdom with the Jewish law.

Old Testament Wisdom Literature

From the standpoint of literary style, the wisdom books of the Old Testament may be divided into two

capital A: Apocrypha (Plural in form and w/c singular use). The 14 books of the Septuagint included in the Vulgate but considered uncanonical by Protestants because they are not part of the Hebrew Scriptures.

8

large categories: books which deal with a wide variety of subjects primarily by means of short maxims (Proverbs), and books which deal with one major theme in a coherent fashion (Job and Ecclesiastes). But all of these works share a common concern: human life. They deal with man's relationship to God, problems of everyday living, motivations, behavior, and destiny. Thus they contain lessons which are of utmost importance for modern man, in fact, for man of any age. (For convenience, the present volume will also include a brief treatment of Song of Solomon, which technically does not belong to the category of Wisdom Literature, but nevertheless communicates a significant message not unlike that found in Proverbs 5-7.)

The basic concern in the book of Job is whether a fundamentally righteous man who experiences tremendous suffering without any apparent reason can still serve God. Can one worship a God who would allow such injustices to exist in the world which he created? Does not a righteous person have every right to expect a reward for his goodness? The central focus in Ecclesiastes is how to cope with the routine weariness of daily life. What purpose could there possibly be in the never ending repetition of days and months and seasons and years, and life which has no alternative but to live in this fixed context? The Song of Solomon extols the joy of sexual and emotional love between man and wife. It praises the merits of marriage as a kind of illustration of the beautiful picture of the coming together of the first man and the first woman under God's guidance in Genesis 2:18-25. The book of Proverbs deals with a wide variety of subjects, including just governmental and business practices, different relationships within the family, the tongue, the nature of true wisdom, and many others. These themes will be developed in a more in-depth manner in the lessons to follow.

Review Questions

1. Compare the role and work of the "wise men" and "wise women" of Israel with that of the priests, prophets, and kings. See Jeremiah 8:8; 18:18; Isaiah 29:14; Proverbs 22:17; 24:23; II Samuel 14:1-24; 20:14-22. Why do you think all these groups were needed to carry out God's purposes in Israel?

2. List nations other than Israel mentioned in the Bible who had "wise men" or "wise women." Judges 5:29; Zechariah 9:2; Obadiah 8; Daniel 2:24; Esther 1:13; Genesis 41:8; Proverbs 30:1. How do you explain this?

3. List the different writings of Egyptian wisdom literature mentioned in this lesson, and tell what is in each. As a class project, read selected portions of some of these works from J. B. Pritchard, *Ancient Near Eastern Texts*, in order to get an idea of what they say and how they say it.

4. List the works belonging to Mesopotamian wisdom literature discussed in this lesson, and tell briefly the contents of each. Again, read selected portions of some of these in class.

5. Name the three apocryphal books which are categorized as wisdom literature, and describe briefly what is in each. Read selected sections from each of these from a good translation of the Apocrypha, such as the RSV.

6. What three things can one learn from comparing Old Testament wisdom literature with ancient extra-biblical wisdom literature? Discuss.

7. What is the major theme of each of the following books?
   a. Job.
   b. Ecclesiastes.
   c. Song of Solomon.
   What are some of the major emphases in the book of Proverbs?

Lesson II

FEAR GOD AND DEPART FROM EVIL

"Behold, the fear of the Lord, that is wisdom;
and to depart from evil is understanding" (Job 28:28).

The main reason the Old Testament books of Job,
Proverbs, and Ecclesiastes, and other works from the
ancient Near East fundamentally similar to them, are
called "wisdom literature" is that they have a great deal
to say about "wisdom." For example, Job 28 contains a
beautiful poem on man's search for wisdom, in which
Job asks:

"But where shall wisdom be found?
And where is the place of understanding?" (verse 12).

And Again:

"Whence then comes wisdom:
And where is the place of understanding?" (verse 20).

The wise man in Proverbs says:

"Happy is the man who finds wisdom,
and the man who gets understanding" (Proverbs 3:13).

And the author of Ecclesiastes declares: "But I say that
wisdom is better than might, though the poor man's
wisdom is despised, and his words are not heeded"
(Ecclesiastes 9:16).

The Meaning of Wisdom

The words "wisdom" and "wise" have a wide variety of
nuances in the Bible, and it is necessary to determine
passage by passage what meaning is intended. (a) Some-

times to be "wise" means to be "skilled" in a particular art or craft, as a seamstress spinning cloth or sewing (Exodus 35:25) or a carpenter building a structure (Exodus 31:6-9; 35:10-18; 36:1; I Kings 7:14; I Corinthians 3:10) or a silversmith forging an idol (Isaiah 40:20) or a sailor handling a ship in rough waters (Ezekiel 27:8; Psalm 107:23-27) (in several of these passages the RSV translates the Hebrew or Greek words for "wisdom" and "wise" by "ability" or "skilled"). (b) This term can also be used of "discretion" or "good judgment" in running the affairs of state, as in the case of Joseph (Genesis 41:33), David (II Samuel 14:20), Solomon (I Kings 3:9,12,28), and kings in general (Proverbs 20:26). Here it should be noted that a major theme which permeates I Kings 3-11 is Solomon's "wisdom." And it is clear from the various settings in which this term is used that it refers to different facets of Solomon's activities. Solomon is said to be "wise" in that he governs Israel well (3:2), shows his ability to reach a right verdict in a court trial (3:28), utters proverbs and songs (4:29-34), carries out a great building program including the building of the temple (10:4), has a very efficient governmental organization, provides for the needs of his subjects, worships the Lord regularly (10:4-5), and answers hard questions put to him by his own subjects and foreigners (10:3, 6-8, 23-24). (c) "Wise" can also carry the sense of "shrewd, crafty, or cunning." Here it can be used with a bad connotation (II Samuel 13:3; Job 5:13; I Corinthians 3:19) or a good one (Matthew 10:16). (d) This word can mean "know how," as in demonstrating a knack to avert wrath (Proverbs 16:14; 29:8,11), or being experienced at doing evil (Jeremiah 4:22) or good (Romans 16:19). (e) "Wisdom" sometimes connotes the idea of being "sharp, smart, intelligent" (Hosea 14:9; Psalm 107:43). (f) Further, "wise men" is a term used of Egyptian (Genesis 41:8,24; Exodus 7:11,22; 8:7; 18-19; 9:11) and Babylonian (Daniel 1:20; 2:2, 12-14, 27; 4:7; 5:7,11-12, 14-15) magicians, sorcerers, and enchanters. (g) "Wisdom" is sometimes synonymous with understanding (Job 12:2-3; 26:3; 38:36).

The Fear of God

But the most fundamental and pervasive meaning of "wisdom" in the Bible and particularly in the Old Testament Wisdom Literature is to "fear God." This is clear from a number of passages.

"The fear of the Lord is the beginning of wisdom, and the knowledge of the Holy One is insight"
(Proverbs 9:10).

"The fear of the Lord is the beginning of knowledge; fools despise wisdom and instruction" (Proverbs 1:7).

"The fear of the Lord is instruction in wisdom, and humility goes before honor" (Proverbs 15:33).

"The fear of the Lord is the beginning of wisdom; a good understanding have all those who practice it"
(Psalm 111:10).

Now these passages do not mean that "wisdom" is like a flight of steps which one must climb in life and the first step is the fear of the Lord, from which one must take a second step to another virtue. Rather, the word "beginning" here means "kernel, core, heart, essence." In other words, essentially the wisdom which God says man needs is the fear of God. This is made quite clear in Job 28:28:

"Behold, the fear of the Lord, *that is wisdom;* and to depart from evil is understanding."

But in passages like these, fearing God is a good thing. It is not something to be avoided or repulsed, nor is it something to be superseded. Rather, it is that to which all who wish to serve God must aspire. Like the word "wisdom," the word "fear" has a variety of meanings in scripture. Therefore, one must be careful to distinguish between different types of fear which are incompatible with godly living and the kind of fear which is essential to a right relationship with God.

13

(1) Accordingly, it should be stressed first of all that the fear which God commends cannot be the same kind of fear experienced by ungodly persons who are not serving God or attempting to do so. When the armies of Syria under Rezin and Israel under Pekah invaded Judah during the reign of Ahaz, Isaiah urged the Jews: "Do not call conspiracy all that this people call conspiracy, and *do not fear what they fear*, nor be in dread. But the Lord of hosts, him you shall regard as holy; *let him be your fear*, and let him be your dread" (Isaiah 8:12-13). When the disciples saw Jesus walking on the water late at night, "they were terrified, saying, 'It is a ghost!' And they cried out for fear. But immediately he spoke to them, saying, 'Take heart, it is I; have no fear'" (Matthew 14:26-27). Further, the author of the book of Hebrews writes: "Keep your life free from love of money, and be content with what you have; for he has said, 'I will never fail you nor forsake you.' Hence we can confidently say,

'The Lord is my helper,
I will not be afraid;
what can man do to me?'" (Hebrews 13:5-6).

Many other examples could be given. But the point is clear. To fear God does not mean to be terrified of him, to cower before him, or to be "scared to death" of him. Jesus, who was God in the flesh, demonstrated over and over again that he wanted men to feel comfortable and at ease around him, to come to him for all kinds of help, and to accept his open arms of welcome to find rest and peace (see Matthew 11:28-30).

(2) Second, the fear which God commends does not mean that one is to live in constant dread that some terrible calamity or affliction or disease is soon to come upon. "Dame Wisdom" promises:

personification

"He who listens to me will dwell secure
    and will be at ease, without dread of evil."
                                    (Proverbs 1:33)

14

And Peter encourages Christians: "Now who is there to harm you if you are zealous for what is right? But even if you do suffer for righteousness' sake, you will be blessed. Have no fear of them, nor be troubled, but in your hearts reverence Christ as Lord" (I Peter 3:13-15a). In light of these truths, it is obvious that "fearing God" is something quite different from "fearing calamity." I John 4:18 is to be understood in this context: "There is no fear in love, but perfect love casts out fear. For *fear has to do with punishment,* and he who fears is not perfected in love." John here certainly is not contrasting love with fearing God, but with fearing punishment or affliction. Fearing God is perfectly compatible with loving God; in fact, properly understood they are identical.

Third, the fear which God commends is not the fear of standing before God in judgment and being consigned to eternity in hell. This kind of fear characterizes one who has never come into covenant relationship with God, or, having done so, has fallen back into his old way of sin; but "fearing God" characterizes him who is faithful to him and serves him constantly. The author of the book of Hebrews makes this point clear when he writes: "For *if we sin deliberately* after receiving the knowledge of the truth, there no longer remains a sacrifice for sins, but a fearful prospect of judgment, and a fury of fire which will consume the adversaries" (Hebrews 10:26-27). Note that those who are said to fear in this passage are not persons faithful to the Lord, but Christians who have deliberately chosen to return to a life of sin.

The Biblical Definition of "Fear"

Of course, the Bible is not a dictionary. Yet there are times when it defines words so that the reader cannot fail to understand their meaning. It does this by using synonymous words in parallel lines in poetry, and by the way it uses words in context. This is the case with the word "fear."

To fear God is to "stand in awe of" him. God condemns the Jewish priests in the days of Malachi by saying: "My covenant with him (that is Levi — see verse 4)
was a covenant of life and peace, and I gave them to
him, that he might fear; and he *feared* me, he *stood in
awe of* my name" (Malachi 2:5). The psalmist writes:

"You who *fear* the Lord praise him!
all you sons of Jacob, glorify him,
and *stand in awe of* him, all you
sons of Israel!" (Psalm 22:23).

To fear God is to give "reverence or honor" to him. In
speaking of the attitude a child should have toward his
parents, all these terms are used. For example, one of
the Ten Commandements is: "*Honor* your father and your
mother" (Exodus 20:12; Deuteronomy 5:16; Matthew 19:19;
Ephesians 6:2). But Leviticus 19:3 (ASV) words it this
way: "Ye shall *fear* every man his mother, and his
father" (the RSV has "revere"). And Hebrews 12:9
(ASV) states: "Furthermore, we had the fathers of our
flesh to chasten us, and we *gave* them *reverence*" (the
RSV says, "we *respected* them"). But a psalmist compares
God's relationship to his people with that of a father to
his children in these terms:

"As a father pities his children,
so the Lord pities those who *fear* him" (Psalm 103:13).

To fear God is to "respect him or to regard him highly."
When Moses announced that God would send hail on the
land of Egypt, there were two responses. "He who *feared*
the word of the Lord among the servants of Pharaoh
made his slaves and his cattle flee into the houses; but
he who did not *regard* the word of the Lord left his
slaves and his cattle in the field" (Exodus 9:20-21). Jesus
begins his parable of the (importunate) widow by saying:
"In a certain city there was a judge who neither *feared*
God nor *regarded* man" (Luke 18:2; see also verse 4). In
Paul's instructions to Christians as to how they were to

*stubbornly or unreasonably persistent
in request or demand* 16

conduct themselves toward civil authorities, he said: "Render to all their dues: . . . *fear* to whom *fear*; *honor* to whom *honor*" (Romans 13:7—ASV; in the former line the RSV has *"respect* to whom *respect* is due").

Biblical Examples of "Fear"

Perhaps the best way to understand the kind of fear God commends in his word is to note the examples of relationships used in the Bible which are linked by the term "fear." There are at least five such relationships.

(1) A slave is to fear his master. Now, of course, this example could indicate that "fear" means to "dread, be terrified by, cower before," and the like, if the master under consideration were harsh and demanding. But the Bible speaks of two kinds of masters: one who is harsh, and one who is kind and gentle. The Lord belongs to the latter type. Paul instructs Christian slaves at Ephesus: "Slaves, be obedient to those who are your earthly masters, *with fear and trembling,* in singleness of heart, *as to Christ;* not in the way of eyeservice, as menpleasers, but *as servants of Christ,* doing the will of God from the heart, rendering service with a good will *as to the Lord* and not to men" (Ephesians 6:5-7). So similarly I Peter 2:18-20. Now surely some of these Christian slaves had harsh non-Christian masters (I Peter 2:18 makes this quite clear). But the motivation for a slave to serve his master here is not fear of punishment if he does not, but faithful commitment to Christ which naturally issues in hard work for one's master. Certainly one is not to conclude from this that Christ is like a harsh, overbearing master, and so the Christian must serve him for fear of being punished. In view of this background, God's words to the Jews in the days of Malachi are very instructive: "A son *honors* his father, and a *servant* his master. If then I am a father, where is my *honor?* and if I am a master, where is my *fear?*" (Malachi 1:6). Further, God calls Job "my *servant,*" and describes him as one "who *fears* God" (Job 1:8; 2:3; cf. 1:1).

17

(2) A citizen is to fear the king or a governmental official. When the Israelites had successfully crossed the Jordan on dry land and set up the stones in commemoration of this momentous event, the Bible states: "On that day Jehovah magnified Joshua in the sight of all Israel; and they *feared* him, as they *feared* Moses, all the days of his life" (Joshua 4:14—ASV; the RSV has "stood in awe of"). After Solomon had settled the dispute between the two harlots, each of whom claimed the living child was hers, by ordering that it be cut in half with a sword, the Bible says: "And all Israel heard of the judgment which the king had judged; and they *feared* the king: for they saw that the wisdom of God was in him, to do justice" (I Kings 3:28—ASV; the RSV translates "stood in awe of"). One may also compare Romans 13:7. Surely these passages do not mean God's people dreaded or were terrified by or cowered before Moses or Joshua or Solomon, but rather that they held them in the highest respect. In a similar way, God wants his people to hold him in the highest respect.

(3) A child is to fear his parents. This point has already been treated above in connection with the thought that "fear" means "reverence or honor" (where Leviticus 19:3; Hebrews 12:9; Psalm 103:13; and other passages were cited). Again, the nuance of respect and honor is clearly intended, and not dread. God wants his children to hold him in the highest regard.

(4) A wife is to fear her husband. Paul tells the Ephesian Christians: "Let the wife see that she *fear* her husband" (Ephesians 5:33—ASV; the RSV has "respects"). Similarly, Peter admonishes, "In like manner, ye wives, be in subjection to your own husbands; that, even if any obey not the word, they may without the word be gained by the behavior of their wives; beholding your chaste behavior coupled with *fear*" (I Peter 3:1-2—ASV; the RSV reads, "when they see your *reverent* and chaste behavior"). Surely the thought is not that the wife is to be "scared to death" of her husband, but rather that she

18

is to respect him highly. God as the husband of Israel, and Christ as the husband of the church, each desires similar honor from his bride.

(5) Jesus feared God. Referring to Christ's difficult ordeal in the garden of Gethsemane shortly before his arrest, trial, and crucifixion, the writer of Hebrews reflects: "In the days of his flesh, Jesus offered up prayers and supplications, with loud cries and tears, to him who was able to save him from death, and he was heard for his godly *fear*" (Hebrews 5:7). Certainly the thought here is not that Jesus dreaded his Father or was terrified of him or cowered before him, but that he held him in the highest respect or honored him.

These examples confirm the biblical definition of "fear" when it is commended to man as the way in which God wants man to live. It means to stand in awe of God, to reverence and honor him, to respect him and hold him in the highest regard.

The Fruits of Fearing God

If a person truly honors God, holds him in the highest respect, stands in awe of him, and reverences him, this fundamental attitude of heart will naturally produce certain specific external fruits in his life. These are made quite clear in scripture, especially in the wisdom literature.

A. One who fears God does God's will by *keeping his commandments*. After wrestling with the meaning and purpose of life, the author of Ecclesiastes ends his book with the affirmation: "The end of the matter; all has been heard. *Fear God, and keep his commandments;* for this is the whole duty of man" (Ecclesiastes 12:13).

B. One who fears God naturally spends his days *serving God*. Joshua's final charge to the people of Israel before his death was: "Now therefore *fear the Lord, and serve him* in sincerity and in faithfulness" (Joshua 24:14).

C. One who fears God continually strives to *do what is right*. Peter begins his sermon to the household of Cornelius by saying: "Truly I perceive that God shows no partiality, but in every nation any one who *fears him and does what is right* is acceptable to him" (Acts 10:34-35).

D. One who fears God *departs from evil*. This is the thought repeated often in the wisdom literature. After all, he who acknowledges God as the most important thing in life hardly has room in his heart and life for evil thoughts, words, and actions. Job declares:

"Behold, *the fear of the Lord*, that is wisdom;
and to *depart from evil* is understanding" (Job 28:28).

Several proverbs declare the same truth.

"Be not wise in your own eyes;
fear the Lord, and turn away from evil" (Proverbs 3:7).

"*The fear of the Lord is hatred of evil*.
Pride and arrogance and the way of evil
and perverted speech I hate" (Proverbs 8:13).

"A wise man *feareth, and departeth from evil;*
But the fool beareth himself insolently,
and is confident" (Proverbs 14:16—ASV).

"By loyalty and faithfulness iniquity is ⟨atoned⟩ stoned for,
and by *the fear of the Lord* a man *avoids evil*"
(Proverbs 16:6)

In light of the biblical teachings emphasized in this lesson, it is very important to realize that in the first two chapters of the book of Job the inspired writer (1:1) and God himself (1:8; 2:3) describe Job as a man "who fears God, and turns away from evil." In other words, Job is a wise man in the best sense of the term. The next few lessons deal with a portion of this man's life revealed in the book of Job.

Review Questions

1. Give seven different meanings of the word "wisdom" in the Bible, with at least one passage which demonstrates each meaning. How does one determine the various nuances of a word?

2. In the statement, "the fear of the Lord is the beginning of wisdom" (Proverbs 9:10, Psalm 111:10), what is meant by the word "beginning"? Discuss.

3. State three things which cannot be meant by "the fear of the Lord" which the Bible commends. Isaiah 8:12-13; Proverbs 1:33; Hebrews 10:26-27. Discuss the meaning of I John 4:18 in light of this.

4. Name two ways one can determine the meaning of "the fear of the Lord" in the Bible.

5. List the terms which are used in parallelism with "fear" in the Bible. Malachi 2:5; Leviticus 19:3 and Hebrews 12:9; Exodus 9:20-21. Discuss each of these terms at length. In light of this, what is meant by "the fear of the Lord" which the Bible commends?

6. Enumerate five biblical examples of relationships in which the word "fear" links the two parties in the relationship. Ephesians 6:5-7; Joshua 4:14; Psalm 103:13; Ephesians 5:33; Hebrews 5:7. In view of this, how would you define "the fear of the Lord" in the positive sense?

7. What are four fruits which "the fear of the Lord" produces in a person's life? Ecclesiastes 12:13; Joshua 24:14; Acts 10:34-35; Job 28:28. Discuss each of these.

8. How do the following passages describe the man Job when he is first introduced in the book of Job? Job 1:1,8; 2:3. Discuss the meaning of these statements made about Job in preparation for the following lessons.

THE TRIALS OF A MAN WHO WAS HEALTHY, WEALTHY, AND WISE (JOB 1-3)

"You have heard of the steadfastness of Job" (James 5:11)

Lessons III-VIII deal with the religious teaching of the book of Job. Because of the nature of this booklet, no attempt is made to discuss critical problems such as the nature of the book, date, authorship, location of the land of Uz, nationality of Job, and so forth. In order to attain a correct understanding of the religious teaching of the book of Job, first it is necessary to lay down some basic principles which one must use in approaching this book, or for that matter, any biblical book.

Some Basic Principles for Interpreting the Bible

The Bible is "inspired by God" (II Timothy 3:16). Among other things, this means that what inspired writers recorded is true and reliable as they recorded it and intended it to be understood under the guidance of and in harmony with the purposes of the Holy Spirit (see II Peter 1:19-21). But this does not mean they agreed with or approved of or commended to their readers everything they recorded. For example, various biblical passages relate the words or deeds of Satan. But this must not be construed to mean God intends for man to follow the devil's example, or that the words the devil speaks are trustworthy. The inspiration of the Bible means that when the Bible says Satan did or said something, he really did so. The same is true of human beings. The inspired author of II Samuel 11 records David's adultery with Bathsheba and murder of her husband Uriah, but this does not mean God approves of adultery or murder, or that he is commending the actions of David to the reader as an example to be followed. As a matter of fact, just the opposite is true. Thus the student of the Bible must learn to distinguish between that which God commends and that which he condemns in his word. This is particularly important in approaching the book of Job. There are several charac- ters in this book: God, Satan, Job, Job's wife, Eliphaz, Bildad, Zophar, and Elihu. And these people advocate different beliefs and viewpoints. How can one determine when a certain speaker is right or wrong? Perhaps the following five principles may be helpful in answering this question.

1. It is essential to *study the whole book* of Job, and not merely selected portions of this work. It is easy to reach simple conclusions about Job and his friends from chapters 1-2, and to ignore what the rest of the book says about them, or what thy say in the rest of the book. Furthermore, as one studies the whole book, it is important that he understand what each speaker is saying at the point he is saying it in the course of the discussion, and not to connect his statements at one point with other of his statements at another point when the two do not belong together.

2. *God's evaluation of Job and his friends* must be correct. Before the calamities fell on Job, God declared that he was "a blameless and upright man, who fears God and turns away from evil" (Job 1:8). And after the initial calamities came, he repeated the same thing and added, "he still holds fast his integrity" (2:3). After this, however, the situation changes. Job charges God with making him suffer without just cause (see for example 9:17; 16:11-17), and dares him to meet him in a fair court trial where he would prove that he is innocent and

23

God has been treating him unfairly (see 31:35-37). God's evaluation of Job now is:

"Will you even put me in the wrong?
Will you condemn me that you may be justified?"
(40:8).

Either God misunderstands and misjudges Job here, or Job has tried to show God was wrong in the way he treated him, and has condemned God that he might be justified. Surely the latter is the case. Further, in the early part of the book God does not evaluate Job's friends: Eliphaz, Bildad, and Zophar. But at the end of the book, God says to Eliphaz: "My wrath is kindled against you and against your two friends; for you have not spoken of me what is right, as my servant Job has" (42:7). This suggests that the position of Job's three friends was wrong. God does not mean here Job was absolutely correct; this would contradict his statement about Job in 40:8. But compared with his friends, Job dealt with his calamities in a much better way than they. (For a more detailed discussion, see the following chapters.) Since God does not evaluate Elihu at the end of the book, and since Elihu's position seems to be very close to God's, one can safely assume that God approved of his words.

3. *Observations* made *by the* inspired *author of the book* of Job must be taken seriously. For example, after the first group of disasters (1:13-19), the author states: "In all this Job did not sin or charge God with wrong" (1:22). In other words, neither his thoughts nor his words were ungodly. But after the second series of afflictions (2:7-10), the author declares: "In all this Job did not sin *with his lips*" (2:10). Nothing is said here about what Job was thinking, however. Yet, in the very next chapter Job himself gives a clue as to what he had been thinking even during his years of prosperity before his trials came:

"Every terror that haunted me has caught up with me,
and all that I feared has come upon me"
(Job 3:15—NEB)

Apparently the inspired writer is saying that there came a point in Job's afflictions at which he began to question the justice of God in making (or allowing) him to suffer so severely.

Again, in his introduction of Elihu, the author of the book of Job states that Job's friends "ceased to answer Job, because he was righteous in his own eyes," and that Elihu "was angry at Job because he justified himself rather than God; he was angry also at Job's three friends because they had found no answer, although they had declared Job to be in the wrong" (32:1-3). The way in which this is worded leads one to believe that the inspired writer agrees with Elihu that Job was wrong because he was righteous in his own eyes, and that Job's three friends also were wrong because they declared Job to be wrong without adequately explaining to him why this was the case.

4. It is necessary to *take seriously the statements of all the speakers* in the book. For example, when Job says:

"He (that is, God) crushes me with a tempest,
and multiplies my wounds *without cause*" (9:17),

it is clear that he is charging God with wrongdoing, as God himself states in 40:8. And to accuse God of being unjust is sin. Again, after God's second speech, Job cries out:

"I had heard of thee by the hearing of the ear,
but now my eye sees thee;
therefore *I despise myself*, and *repent* in dust and ashes" (42:5-6).

Obviously Job felt he needed to repent. Was he mistaken, or is that what he really needed to do? A study of the book of Job shows the latter is the case. But if this is so, then Job must have committed sin of which he had to repent. And this would suggest he did so in his speeches recorded in this biblical book. (Note that this, too, conforms with God's statements in 40:8.)

25

5. *Passages* in the Bible *outside the book of Job* must be taken into consideration in evaluating the various speakers in this book. Two passages outside the book of Job refer to Job. (a) One is Ezekiel 14:12-20. Here God declares Judah is so sinful that if Noah, Daniel, and Job were living in her they could not save anyone in the land but themselves "by their righteousness." So the Lord says Job was *righteous*. Does this mean he was *sinless?* In this same text, God says Noah was righteous; yet after the flood Noah "became drunk, and lay uncovered in his tent" (Genesis 8:21). II Peter 2:7-8 describes Lot as "righteous." Yet, when the men of Sodom demanded that he bring out the angels whom he had invited to spend the night in his house that they might know them, Lot replied: "I beg you, my brothers, do not act so wickedly. Behold, I have two daughters who have not known man; let me bring them out to you, and do to them as you please" (Genesis 19:5-8). Such a proposal can hardly be termed righteous. In other words, "righteous" does not mean "sinless." So Job could well be a righteous man, and still commit sin, even in reaction to the sufferings which befell him. (b) James 5:11 also refers to Job. But here it is important to read the entire verse: "You have heard of the steadfastness of Job, and you have seen the purpose of the Lord, how the Lord is compassionate and merciful." The first line fits Job's response to his sufferings recorded in Job 1 (and possibly chapter 2), but not his words in chapters 3 following. But possibly the last line of James 5:11 is still talking about Job. If so, it is saying that God showed Job compassion and mercy. But this assumes Job committed sin, or else he would not need the Lord's compassion and mercy. This concept would fit Elihu's description of the way God works with man (Job 33:14-30), and also the account of Job's repentance and God's blessings on him in the final chapter.

Job Before His Trials (1:1-5)

When the Bible first introduces Job, he seems to be a man of approximately fifty-five to sixty years of age, because he had ten children (seven sons and three daughters), all of whom were grown and living in their own homes (verses 2,4). Job lived an additional 140 years after the Lord raised him up (42:16), during which time he had ten more children (42:13). So he lived approximately 200 years. The longevity of his life and his capacity to bear children suggest he was a very *healthy* person.

Job had "seven thousand sheep, three thousand camels, five hundred yoke of oxen, and five hundred she-asses, and very many servants; so that this man was the greatest of all the people of the east" (1:3). The context makes it quite clear that "greatest" is to be understood in the sense of "wealthiest." So Job was a very *wealthy* person.

Job was also a man who "feared God, and turned away from evil" (1:1,8; 2:3). But this is the standard description of the *wise* man in Old Testament wisdom literature (cf. 28:28 and the previous lesson in this booklet). He held God in the highest respect. As an example of this, when his grown children held a family feast, Job would offer burnt offerings in behalf of them all for fear they might have sinned and cursed God in their hearts (1:5).

Thus the Bible first introduces Job as one who was "healthy, wealthy, and wise." But lest one be misled, two observations are in order. (1) The affirmation that Job was "blameless (some versions read perfect) and upright" does not mean he was sinless. Titus 1:6 says an elder must be blameless, Philippians 2:15 says a Christian must be blameless, and Jesus says in the Sermon on the Mount that his followers must be perfect as God is perfect (Matthew 5:48). Since "all have sinned and fall short of the glory of God" (Romans 3:23), it is inconceivable that God or Christ requires of man sinlessness. Rather, "blameless" connotes purity of motive and childlike innocence, and "perfect" means "mature, full-grown."

(2) Whether consciously or subconsciously, Job was very concerned not only to *be* righteous, but also to make sure that his righteousness was *recognized and appreciated*. This is amply demonstrated in his speeches throughout the heart of the book. In fact, some of his favorite assertions are: "I am innocent" or "I am blameless" or "I am not guilty," and the like (cf. 9:15,20,21; 10:7; 12:4; 13:18,23; 16:17; 19:4,7; 23:1C-12; 27:5-6; 31:1-40). Apparently it was this attitude of Job that God sought to remove by approaching Satan and challenging him to test Job's faith (for a detailed discussion, see Lessons VII and VIII).

God and Satan (1:6-12; 2:1-6)

There are several events in both the Old and New Testaments in which both God and Satan are said to have worked. A few examples may suffice. (1) II Samuel 24:1 states *the Lord* "incited David" against Israel, while the parallel account in I Chronicles 21:1 says *Satan* did this. (2) Zechariah 3:1-2 describes how *the Lord* rebuked *Satan* who stood at the right hand of Joshua the high priest to accuse him. (3) Matthew 4:1 states that Jesus was led up *by the Spirit* into the wilderness to be tempted *by the devil.* (4) Paul states that his "thorn in the flesh" was given him by *the Lord,* whom he besought thrice that it should leave him, but he also identifies that thorn as a messenger of *Satan* (II Corinthians 12:7-10). (5) John 13:2 says *the devil* put it into the heart of Judas to betray Jesus — thus Satan was active in putting Christ on the cross. But Peter declares on Pentecost that Jesus was delivered up and crucified "according to the definite plan and foreknowledge of *God"* (Acts 2:23).

Certain specific conclusions may be drawn from these examples which will aid in properly understanding the functions of God and Satan in Job 1-2. First, it is possible for both God and Satan to work in the same event; yet, this does not mean they are cooperating or that they have the same purposes and goals in mind.

28

God's purposes are good, but Satan's are destructive. Second, events or conditions which seem bad to man, such as setbacks, failure, suffering, and even death, may not necessarily be bad at all. God may use these things as means of accomplishing his purposes, and of forming man into the kind of person he wants him to be and he should be. Third, it is very important that God, and not Satan, be given credit for actively working in affairs which produce good. For example, if one attributes Christ's death on the cross to Satan and disavows God's active role in that event, then Satan is responsible for man's salvation. Or, if Satan is the one who gave Paul his thorn in the flesh and God had nothing to do with it, then Satan is to be praised for "keeping Paul from being too elated" (II Corinthians 12:7), that is, from being proud.

In light of this, one cannot be satisfied simply with the explanation that God "allowed" or "permitted" Satan to afflict Job, although this is *partly* the case (1:9-12; 2:4-6). The biblical text states that God did more than merely play a *passive* role in Job's trials. On the contrary, in both conversations with the devil, God *actively* takes the initiative and challenges Satan to afflict Job, saying: "Have you considered my servant Job, that there is none like him on the earth, a blameless and upright man, who fears God and turns away from evil?" (1:8, 2:3). And in the second instance, he "rubs it in" to the devil by adding: "He still holds fast his integrity, although you moved me against him to destroy him without cause" (see further 42:11).

In view of the whole book of Job, there seems to be at least two reasons why God issues such a challenge. (a) He has confidence in Job. Although Job may have difficulty in dealing with these trials and fall under their weight, ultimately God is persuaded he will come out on top. What a compliment to know that God trusts in his servants. (b) God knows that Job needs suffering in order to grow spiritually as he should. The feelings these afflictions bring out in Job's heart, the complaints and contentions against God which they evoke from Job's mouth, and Job's ultimate repentance, all show their value to him.

The picture which Job 1 and 2 paint of God and Satan makes it quite clear that they are not equals, but that Satan is totally subject to God. Since God is the source of all power in the universe, the devil acknowledges that he must use a part of that power to afflict Job. So he asks God: "Put forth thy hand now, and touch all that he has" (1:11), or later, "Put forth thy hand now, and touch his bone and his flesh" (2:5). And God himself says to Satan: "*You moved me against him*" (2:3). Here power and free will come into play, as they always do in relationships involving God and the rational creatures he has made, whether angels or men. No creature of God can do anything without using the power or energy God supplies, but God has made his creatures so that they are free to use his power as they choose, even to disobey him, yet within the limits which he prescribes by his wisdom. So, for example, using the power which God provides, Assyria may decide to march against Judah to *destroy* her; however, God uses Assyria to punish his people for their sins, but refuses to allow her to destroy them (Isaiah 10:5-7, 12-15).

Job's Trials (1:13-19; 2:7-10b, 11-13)

The trials Job experiences come in two waves: the first consisting of four specific events, and the second of three, making a total of seven afflictions.

The first four calamities affect "all that he (Job) has" (1:11), "his possessions" (1:10), that is, his *wealth*. These come with such rapidity that Job hardly has time to absorb one before he learns of another. And each time Job loses something more precious to him than the one before. (1) The Sabeans seize his oxen and asses and kill the servants in charge of them (1:14-15). (2) Lightning ("the fire of God") kills his sheep and shepherds (1:16). (3) Three companies of Chaldeans confiscate his camels and kill their keepers (1:17). (4) A great wind (the sirocco) strikes the house in which Job's ten children are holding a feast and kills all of them (1:18-19; cf. verse 4).

The next three afflictions are more subtle, and attack Job's *health* (number 5) and *wisdom* (numbers 6 and 7). (5) Job is afflicted with loathsome sores all over his body so that he has to sit among the ashes and scrape himself with a potsherd (2:7-8). (6) After watching her husband suffer perhaps for several months (cf. 7:3; 30:16), Job's wife can no longer bear to watch him in such great pain and urges him to "curse God and die" (2:9). (7) Job's three friends (Eliphaz, Bildad, and Zophar) come from rather distant lands in order to comfort Job, but when they see how terrible he looks (they do not even recognize him; see Isaiah 52:14) and how great his suffering is, they sit with him in silence for seven days and seven nights (2:11-13). As it was customary to spend seven days mourning for the dead (cf. Genesis 50:10; I Samuel 31:13), evidently the friends were holding their own funeral for Job under the assumption that he would certainly die very soon and they could not come to the funeral because their homes were too far away for such to be practical. What Job needed so desperately was not silence or advise or condemnation, but some sympathetic understanding — and on this point everyone around failed him.

Job's Initial Responses to these Trials (1:20-22; 2:10; 3)

Apparently there is a gradual progression from trusting resignation to God's will to an anguished rejection of any desire to be alive in Job's reactionary feelings to his trials. In response to the first four calamities, he boldly resigns himself to the condition which God has brought upon him. After all, he realized that all of his possessions were gifts from God, and that any time God wished he could take these gifts away from him. So he

31

worshiped God and said: "The Lord gave, and the Lord has taken away; blessed be the name of the Lord" (1:21). Later, when he is smitten with a terrible disease and his wife finally urged him to curse God and die, he chides her for speaking as one of the "foolish" women speak, and says people must receive evil (calamity) at the Lord's hand with grace as well as good (blessing); yet the author's statement, "in all this Job did not sin *with his lips*" (2:10), may suggest he had begun to doubt God's justice in treating him so severely. Finally, after Job's three friends offer him no comfort as they sit in silence about him, he blurts out passionately that he wishes he had never been born (3:1-10), that he had died at birth (3:11-15) or in his mother's womb (3:16-19), and prays fervently that he might die (3:20-26; see Jeremiah 20:14-18). He confesses that while he was prospering, he wondered if it was all too good to be true, and now his afflictions bear out his fears.

"Every terror that haunted me has caught up with me, and all that I feared has come upon me" (3:25—NEB).

(see on this Proverbs 10:24).

In spite of the obvious severity of Job's suffering, it is clear that he has now reached the "breaking point." God is not pleased with the attitude, "God should never have created me, and now that life has become hard for me and it is not going my way, I want to die." In fact, it amounts to saying: "God failed or did something wrong when he created me, and is now failing or doing wrong by causing or allowing my present afflictions." This attitude calls to mind that of Elijah (I Kings 19:4) and of Jonah (Jonah 4:3,8-9). It may be that others would do no better than Job under the same or similar circumstances, but this does not remove the fact that his attitude here is sinful.

These considerations bring into sharp focus the real issue in the book of Job. Ironically it is stated succinctly and pointedly by Satan in his reply to God's initial challenge: "Does Job fear God for nought?" (1:9). In other words, why does man serve God? Why does he worship him? Why is he faithful to him? Might it be for selfish reasons? Is it in order to maintain his health and live a long life, to increase his wealth and possessions and enjoy the respect and goodwill of his wife and children, and to sustain a good reputation among his friends and in the world at large? Or can a person, will a person, should a person, serve God even if all these things are taken away from him — without any apparent reason or justification? Will he remain faithful to his creator even if his circumstances are filled with "good reasons" to doubt and even denounce the way God is dealing with him? Will he worship God, just because God above is worthy of praise and honor, or in order to receive God's blessings? This is what is at stake in the book of Job.

Review Questions

1. Does the affirmation that the Bible is the inspired word of God mean that God and the inspired writers agreed with and commended all that they recorded? Discuss.

2. List the five principles suggested in this lesson for evaluating the different speakers in the book of Job. Discuss each of these, and their implications for understanding the book of Job. Can you think of additional principles which should be applied?

3. What three terms best describe Job before his calamities came upon him? Was Job sinless? See Romans 3:23. Discuss.

4. Name five events cited in the Bible in which both God and Satan were actively at work. II Samuel 24:1 and I Chronicles 21:1; Zechariah 3:1-8; Matthew 4:1-11; II Corinthians 12:7-10; John 13:2 and Acts 2:23. List the three conclusions which can be drawn from this as suggested in this lesson, and show how this is relevant to understanding Job 1-2.

5. What were the first four calamities which came upon Job? Job 1:13-19. How did Job respond to these? Job 1:20-22. What great lesson can the modern Christian learn from this?

6. What was the fifth trial Job suffered? Job 2:7-8. How did Job's wife respond to this? Job 2:9. What subtle sixth trial did this pose for Job? How did Job respond to this? Job 2:10.

7. What was the seventh problem Job faced? Job 2:11-13. Why did this pose a problem for him? How did Job respond to this? Job 3. Evaluate Job's statements in chapter 3. Do you think what Job is saying here is sinful or not? See I Kings 19:4; Jonah 4:3, 8-9. Discuss.

Lesson IV

DO ALL RIGHTEOUS PEOPLE PROSPER AND ALL WICKED PEOPLE SUFFER? (Job 4-5, 8, 11, 15, 18, 20, 22, 25)

"Behold, God will not reject a blameless man, nor take the hand of evildoers" (Job 8:20).

Because of the nature of the book of Job and of the present volume, the approach to Job 4-31 will not be to follow the speeches of the various speakers in the order in which they appear in the book. However, the comments which are made endeavor to take very seriously the context in which the different points are made, and the place in the sequence of the speeches at which they come. For example, in Eliphaz's first speech (chapters 4-5), he praises Job for helping the poor and suffering (4:3-4); but in his last speech (chapter 22), he condemns Job for treating the poor and suffering very harshly (22:5-9). Such changes in a speaker's position will be noted in the discussion to follow. In order that the various speeches may be viewed at their proper place in the book, the following outline of speakers may prove helpful.

I. The first series in the debate—4-14.
  A. Eliphaz's first speech—4-5.
  B. Job's reply—6-7.
  C. Bildad's first speech—8.
  D. Job's reply—9-10.
  E. Zophar's first speech—11.
  F. Job's reply—12-14.
II. The second series in the debate—15-21.
  A. Eliphaz's second speech—15.

no 3rd for Zophar!

This lesson deals with the position of Eliphaz, Bildad, and Zophar. Attempts have been made to distinguish between these three individuals. For example, Eliphaz has been described as the "prophet" of his time, the oldest, most learned, and most sympathetic toward Job of the three; Bildad, as the "sage" of his time, who had profound admiration for his forefathers and was steeped in tradition; and Zophar, as the youngest of the three, who is absolutely certain that he has all the answers to human problems, that truth can be one way and one way alone, and that he is right and cannot be wrong. There may be some merit to such characterizations, but in reality Job's three friends hold basically the same position, and if there were more information about them individually, such descriptions might well appear oversimplified.

Now viewed in light of truths taught elsewhere in the Bible, Eliphaz, Bildad, and Zophar appear to express many correct ideas. However, one must evaluate their thoughts in light of God's statement to Eliphaz at the end of the book: "My wrath is kindled against you and against your two friends; for you have not spoken of me what is right, as my servant Job has" (42:7; see also verse 8). There can be little doubt that Job's friends uttered many truths, but the point is that what they said was not relevant to Job's situation and God's role therein. There is a great difference between correctly stating an abstract truth and applying truth to a real human need.

These thoughts provide a foundation for examining the views of Job's three friends.

The View of Eliphaz (Job 4-5, 15, 22)

The three friends feel compelled to respond to Job's opening speech (chapter 3; cf. 4:2), assuming from their prior long acquaintance with him that he is a righteous man, but at the same time stunned that he would complain so bitterly over his suffering and curse the day of his birth.

Eliphaz's first speech (chapters 4-5) falls into four paragraphs. (1) He praises Job for encouraging and comforting the afflicted, then chides him for not practicing what he preaches. Now that calamity comes on Job, he is "impatient" (4:5). Eliphaz urges him to be confident because of his "fear of God." Job's suffering will be only for a short while, because he is a righteous man, and God does not "cut off" a righteous man, although a little pain may come into his life. Only the sinful will be destroyed.

"As I have seen, those who plow iniquity
and sow trouble reap the same" (4:8) (4:1-11).

In verse 6, Eliphaz inadvertantly states the heart of Job's problem (and indeed, that of the three friends), namely, that the real object of Job's trust is his own goodness, the fact that he is one who "fears God," rather than God himself. The difference between the two is immense, as is beautifully illustrated by Jesus in his parable of the Pharisee and the publican (Luke 18:9-14). (2) Eliphaz claims he saw a night vision in which a spirit declared to him that no mortal man could be righteous before God. Thus Job is in no position to question God's actions, and can expect some suffering because he too is a sinner. Job should not envy the prosperity of the wicked, for at best it is short-lived. Affliction does not come from itself, but is due to man's sin. Thus Job must be responsible for his suffering (4:12-5:7).

37

(3) Eliphaz declares that if he were in Job's place, he would simply assume God knows what he is doing and trust him to restore him to his former health and wealth very soon, because God's ways are beyond man's comprehension, as he continually demonstrates in his works in nature and the lives of men. The same God who has frequently overthrown the mighty and elevated the downtrodden can do it again in Job's case (5:8-16). (4) Eliphaz urges Job to rejoice over his suffering, because it is the means that "the Great Physician," God, is using to remove a fatal, hidden, spiritual cancer from Job's life. By performing this "operation" on Job, God will deliver him from "seven troubles" and restore to him his former prosperity (5:17-27).

The second speech of Eliphaz (chapter 15) falls naturally into three paragraphs. (1) He concludes that if Job is correct in saying many righteous people suffer and many wicked people prosper (cf. 9:22; 12:6), this does away with "the fear of God" (15:4), that is, no one could honor and respect a God like that (15:1-6). (2) Eliphaz rebukes Job for thinking he has the truth and so all the "fathers" were wrong when they concluded the righteous prosper and the wicked suffer. He repeats his former contention (in 4:17-19) that no man, not even Job, is righteous before God, and therefore he is in no position to say God is unjust in making him suffer (15:7-16). (3) Again repeating himself (cf. 5:3-5), Eliphaz affirms that although a wicked man may seem to be prospering, the truth is that he is living in constant fear of losing all his possessions, and in fact he will be destroyed prematurely like a tree whose branch does not become green or a vine whose grapes fall off before they become ripe or an olive tree that casts off its blossoms (15:17-35).

Eliphaz's third speech (chapter 22) also contains three sections. (1) He declares that even if Job were righteous, this would be no profit or benefit to God. But in fact, Job is a rank sinner who has mistreated many helpless people, and (this) is why all his sufferings have come upon him (22:1-11). With this accusation, Eliphaz contradicts his own praise of Job in his first speech for helping those who were afflicted (cf. 4:3-4). (2) Eliphaz states that God punishes the wicked, even though they may prosper temporarily; thus man is in no position to question God's ways (22:12-20). (3) Eliphaz counsels Job to repent and turn to God; then God will hear his prayer and deliver him (22:21-30).

The View of Bildad (Job 8, 18, 25)

The whole philosophy of (Bildad,) like that of his two friends, is that God always blesses the righteous and curses the wicked. He states this succinctly in 8:20:

"Behold, God will not reject a blameless man,
nor take the hand of evildoers."

Bildad's first speech (chapter 8) consists of two paragraphs. (1) God is always just, no matter how things might appear. If Job will but repent, God will reward him well (8:1-7). (2) The "fathers" (former generations), whose wisdom is to be revered, correctly taught that all righteous people prosper and all wicked people suffer. The wicked may prosper for a short time, but they are like papyrus plants which sprout up quickly but are the first to wither (verses 11-13), or like a spider's web which may appear sturdy but can be swept away by one flick of the wrist (verses 14) (8:8-22).

I – Bildad

(untrue, tho')

Bildad's second speech (chapter 18) is a reaffirmation of the unwavering position of the three friends that the wicked always suffer. The fall of the wicked is like the capture of some animal or bird that feels secure and has no indication whatsoever that danger is anywhere near (see especially verses 8-11).

II – Bildad

The (last speech) of Bildad (chapter 25) repeats the friends' position that no man can be righteous before God; rather, he is a "maggot" and a "worm."

III – Bildad

The View of Zophar (Job 11, 20)

Zophar presents only two speeches, and they are very shallow. His first speech (chapter 11) consists of two sections. (1) He declares once again that God always deals justly with man, although man cannot comprehend his ways (11:1-12). As a matter of fact, God has been more than just with Job, as he himself would state if he would only appear. He has been merciful! Thus Zophar says to Job: "Know then that God exacts of you less than your guilt deserves" (verse 6). (2) Zophar urges Job to repent so that God might forgive him of his sins and restore him to health and prosperity (11:13-20).

In his second speech (chapter 20), Zophar restates the position of the friends that a wicked man may prosper for a short while, but he will soon be cut off. His prosperity, gained by wickedness, is like a tasty morsel which someone tries to hold in his mouth as long as he can, but when he soon swallows it, it becomes bitter in his belly (verses 12-15). He is as insecure as a man who successfully flees from an iron weapon only to be slain by bronze arrow (verses 24-25).

Summary of the Friends' Position

A study of the speeches of Job's three friends shows their basic assumption is that all righteous people prosper and all wicked people suffer throughout most of their lives on earth (4:8; 5:2-7, 12-14; 8:11-15, 20; 15:20-34; 18:5-21), though admittedly a righteous person may suffer for a brief time (4:7) and a wicked person may prosper temporarily (5:3-5; 8:11-15; 15:20-24; 18:5-7; 20:5, 23-25; 22:15-16). All their other points are subservient to this basic thesis, and may be reduced to five propositions.

First, the view of the "fathers" or ancestors in former generation is unanimous, invariable, and correct on this issue (8:8-10; 15:10 18; 20:4). This is confirmed by research and discussion among the wise (5:27), by personal experience (4:8; 15:17; 20:2-3), and by a mysterious revelation Eliphaz claims to have been given by a spirit in a night vision (4:12-16). Second, it is certain that if God himself were to appear and speak, he would take precisely this position; so that "when we speak, God speaks," or at least it is the same as if God were speaking (11:5-6; 15:11; 22:21).

Third, God is always just (8:3), even though it is impossible for man to comprehend his ways (11:6-12; 15:7-9). Fourth, no man can be just or righteous before God just because he is human, if for no other reason (4:17-19; 15:14-16; 25:4-6). Fifth, (and growing out of all these other premises), Job must be a great sinner, and therefore his only hope of deliverance is to repent (8:5-7; 11:13-20; 15:1-7; 22:21-30).

At the end of the book of Job, God rebukes Job's three friends, saying, "you have not spoken of me what is right, as my servant Job has" (42:7, 8). The word "as" shows that this is a *relative* evaluation. It does not mean everything Job said was right and everything the friends said was wrong, but that "relatively speaking" Job, and not his friends, was going in the direction of truth. In light of this, perhaps a brief assessment of the friends' position is in order.

1. The view that all righteous people prosper and all wicked people suffer assumes all men are precisely the same, and God responds mechanically to human behavior rather than as one personality to another. A parent's experience with more than one child shows how fallacious this is. Each individual is different, and must be treated in keeping with his own unique personality. It would be unwise and damaging for a parent to treat all his children alike. His treatment of each child must be suited to the needs and temperament of that child. God deals with man in a similar way. Like all who defend a rigid position, Job's friends leave themselves an "escape valve." If a wicked man is prospering, he must be full of agony

within, and his prosperity will be short-lived. Or possibly one who appears to be righeous or wicked is not really so. The position of Job's friends also assumes there must be a logical reason or explanation for everything that happens in life, and that man is capable of understanding that reason. Thus when Eliphaz said:

"As I have seen, those who plow iniquity
and sow trouble reap the same" (4:8),

what he really meant was that what a man reaps indicates clearly what he must have sown. Because Job was suffering, he must have have committed a great sin. Now if one traces this to its logical conclusion, Jesus must have been a great sinner because of the suffering he endured, or when a Christian is persecuted because of his commitment to Christ he must have committed a great sin. Perhaps the greatest fallacy of Job's friends was their insistence on defending their doctrine at all costs, while what Job really needed was their sympathy and understanding.

2. Just because many people have believed something for a long period of time does not prove it is true. For example, it was once believed that the earth was flat, but this did not make is so. Human beliefs may be incorrect, and therefore he who is genuinely seeking truth must be willing to have his beliefs scrutinized at any time. Job's friends did nothing more than "mouth" or "parrot" the views of their ancestors. They were not willing to examine new evidence, or to think for themselves. They had been convinced for years that Job was a righteous man, but they denied this in order to defend their dogma.

3. The friends violently oppose Job's assumption that he knows God's ways, affirming that no man can comprehend what God is doing (11:7-9; 15:7-9). Yet they are quite confident that they fully understand God, and thus their viewpoint is equivalent to God's. What a glaring inconsistency!

42

4. There is a difference between God's being just and man's ability to see, comprehend, and explain his justice. Job's friends assumed that God's justice always means he blesses the righteous and punishes the wicked. Consequently, Job must be wicked because he is suffering.

5. It is ironic that the friends declare no man can be righteous before God, yet apparently view themselves as righteous since they are not suffering.

Many of the points and arguments of Job's friends are true. But they are wrong because they are irrelevant to Job's situation, needs, and position. Valid truth for life is not a correct abstract proposition, but a reality which fits the problem, circumstances, or needs existing in human life at any given time.

Review   Quesitons

1. Make a brief outline of Eliphaz's three speeches. Summarize his major points. Job 4-5, 15, 22.

2. Give the contents of each of Bildad's speeches. State the main points he makes. Job 8, 18, 25.

3. Briefly outline Zophar's two speeches, and list his leading contentions. Job 11, 20.

4. What is the basic argument of Job's three friends? How do they modify it slightly to explain seeming contradictions to their view? Discuss.

5. State the five contentions of Eliphaz, Bildad, and Zophar. Discuss each of these.

6. Point out the fallacies in the position of Job's friends. How should this help modern man understand human life on earth, and the way God deals with man?

Lesson V

IS GOD ARBITRARY?
(Job 6-7, 9-10, 12-14)

"He destroys both the blameless and the wicked"
(Job 9:22)

Lessons V and VI deal with the position of Job in his debate with his three friends. It would be a great mistake to assume that Job's attitudes toward God and his suffering are the same in the debate as they were when the first calamities came upon him (1:20-22), or that they remain consistent throughout the debate. Unlike Eliphaz, Bildad, and Zophar, Job quickly abandons the traditional view and launches out on a sincere search for truth. Before his afflictions came upon him, Job held the same religious position as his friends: all righteous people prosper and all wicked people suffer. But now he is faced with the inescapable reality that he is suffering, and yet he is convinced that he is fundamentally a righteous man and thus does not deserve the severity of suffering to which he is being subjected. As one examines Job's arguments, he should keep in mind that at the end of the book God accuses Job of putting him in the wrong and of condemning him that he might be justified (40:8), Job repents (42:6), and yet God says Job was more "right" than his friends in the way he evaluated and dealt with his sufferings (42:7-8).

Comparatively or relatively speaking (see #5, p 41)

Job's First Response to Eliphaz (Job 6-7).

When he first broke his silence, Job complained because his suffering was so great, bemoaned the fact he had ever been born, and pleaded with God to let him die

45

(chapter 3). Eliphaz then chided him for being "impatient" and not accepting his affliction as he had counseled many others to do (4:3-5). Now Job gives three reasons why his complaining about his suffering and his longing for death are justified, and why he has every right to be impatient. (On this last point, note 6:11:

"What is my strength, that I should wait?
And what is my end, that I should be *patient?*")

1. First, Job declares his suffering is greater than any man could bear. Admittedly he is guilty of sin, as are all men; but his suffering is totally out of proportion to any transgression he may have committed (6:1-13; 7:1-10). In these two paragraphs, Job gives seven illustrations to support his right to complain and to yearn for death under such severe calamities. (1) No man is able to bear such suffering any more than he could carry all the sand of all the beaches of the earth on his back (6:2-3). (2) It is as natural for one suffering so severely to complain as it is for a wild ass to bray or an ox to low when deprived of feed (6:5). (3) Complaining is as necessary to the afflicted as salt is to bland food or the yellow of an egg to the white (6:6-7). (4) Perhaps one could bear such suffering if he were made of "stones" or "bronze," if he were a robot, but man is made of flesh and bones and blood and hair, and thus such great affliction is overwhelming (6:12-13). (5) It is as normal for one stricken with such calamities to yearn for death as it is for a slave hard at work, sweltering under the hot sun, to long for the shadow of a cloud or a tree, or (6) for a hireling whose funds are spent and who has labored hard and steadily to look forward to the day he will be paid (7:1-3). (7) Life is too short for anyone to have to suffer this much. A person's days on earth pass by as quickly as a weaver's shuttle swiftly intertwining strands of thread for making a garment (7:6), the act of inhaling and exhaling — of taking a breath (7:7), and a fleecy cloud evaporating into the atmosphere and disappearing (7:9). And when one dies, he will never return to live again on this earth (7:8-10).

Second, Job affirms that his friends have failed to comfort him in his hour of deepest need (6:14-30). They are like a brook whose waters overflow its banks during the rainy season, but go dry when the hot summer arrives (verses 15-21), or like two creditors bargaining over an orphan child whose parent or parents had been in the debt of both (verse 27).

Third, Job accuses God of bringing unbearable suffering upon him and urges him to tell him "why" (7:11-21). When he tries to get relief through sleep, God terrifies him with dreams and visions. He begs God to leave him alone so he can die and be delivered from his afflictions. If he has sinned, he urges God to forgive him.

Job's First Response to Bildad (Job 9-10)

Bildad had affirmed that God always blesses the righteous and curses the wicked. Job replies that this is not the case with him. He is innocent, but God stubbornly refuses to give him a chance to prove it. Accordingly, he makes three charges against God.

First, God uses his power and wisdom to make a man appear to his fellows as a sinner through his afflictions and to keep man from ever getting an opportunity to prove his innocence (9:1-12, 25-35). Job, like all men, is helpless before God's power and wisdom (9:4). There is no way a man can be just before God, because God will not allow him to "contend with" him, to "answer" him, and prove he is just (9:2-3), since he is able to do whatever he pleases (9:12). No matter how hard Job tries, God is determined to make him look guilty, not to hold him innocent, but to condemn him (9:27-31). The reason for this is that God does not understand man so that they might meet one another in a fair court trial (9:32), and furthermore there is no one who could "umpire" such a lawsuit fairly, explaining man's position to God and God's to man (9:33). If God would just quit terrifying Job by his awesome displays of power and wisdom, he could "speak" with clear mind and prove his innocence, that God is making him suffer without just cause (9:34-35). But Job has no hope of defending himself before God — the contest is unequal. Job is desperate to meet God in a court trial and vindicate himself, because he realizes how rapidly life is fleeting away from him. His days (1) are swifter than a runner (9:25); (2) go by like the light Egyptian skiffs of reed (small boats something like canoes) which skim rapidly across the water; and (3) go by like an eagle swooping on its prey (sometimes reaching a speed of almost a hundred miles an hour, verse 26; for other illustrations of the brevity of life by Job, see 7:6, 7, 9).

Second, Job charges that even though he is "innocent" (9:15, 20, 23) or "blameless" (9:20, 21) of sin which would warrant anything like the suffering he is forced to endure, God is making him suffer "without" just "cause" (9:17) and refuses to allow him an opportunity to defend himself (9:13-24). In other words, God is "arbitrary" in the way he deals with man: "He destroys both the blameless and the wicked" (9:22). He is *unjust*.

Third, Job accuses God of being *inconsistent* in the way he deals with man (chapter 10). He pleads with God to reveal to him *why* he is making him suffer (10:2). It does not make sense for God to go to all the trouble of creating man, only to turn upon him with heavy affliction (10:3, 8-20). Evidently God had planned to afflict Job from the beginning (10:8-15). The longevity of God's life is vastly different from the few years man lives on earth, and thus it is unbecoming of God to try to make man appear sinful by punishing him severely, knowing all the while that he is "not guilty" (10:4-7). Job finds himself in a "no win" situation. If he sins, God will punish him; and if he is righteous, God will punish him (10:14-15). Obviously God is arbitrary. So Job pleads with God to let him die that he might be relieved from his affliction (10:20-22).

Job's First Response to Zophar (Job 12-14)

After Zophar's first speech, reaffirming invariable strict retribution in God's dealings with man, Job first addresses his three friends and tries to refute their fallacious reasoning (12:1-13:19), then addresses God, pleading with him to give him a fair chance to defend himself in a court trial against him (13:20-14:22).

The address to the friends may be divided conveniently into three paragraphs. (1) Job again declares that God is arbitrary (12:1-6). He afflicts the righteous, as Job's own suffering proves (12:4); and blesses the wicked, as prosperous robbers apparently known to Job and to his friends demonstrates (12:6). (2) All creation agrees with one accord that God is all wise and all powerful (12:7-13:2). But he uses this wisdom and power to overwhelm man and make it impossible for him to defend himself if he is treated unjustly. (3) Job rebukes his friends for purporting to support God's position and to be seeking to comfort him, while they have failed on both counts (13:4-14, 17). He yearns for an opportunity to meet God in a court trial before he dies, and to prove he is not guilty of great sins such as his enormous sufferings might lead one to conclude (13:3, 15-16, 18-19).

Job's address to God contains two paragraphs. (1) Job begs God to stop afflicting him so he can think clearly, and then give him a chance to defend himself in a court trial; life is too short for any man to have to continue undergoing the suffering he is experiencing (13:20-14:6). Job is in constant pain because God is relentlessly pursuing him like one would pursue a leaf or dry chaff driven by the wind (13:25), or is keeping him under constant surveillance like an untrusting and suspicious master would do his slave (13:27). Life is much too brief for one to have to suffer so much. It is like a flower that withers, or a shadow which is soon gone (14:2 — for other figures on the brevity of life by Job, see 7:6, 7, 9; 9:25-26).

49

(2) In a surge of desperate fantasy, Job longs for God to let him die and go to Sheol (the realm of the dead, the grave) until his anger at Job subside; then he wishes God would raise him from the dead to live on earth once again, so he could meet God in a court trial and prove his innocence (14:13-17). But Job realizes this is but a wild dream. A tree might be cut down and yet live again on the earth by little shoots springing up from the stump (14:7-9); but when man dies, he will never live again on this earth (14:10, 12, 14, 19-22). He is like water which evaporates from a lake when it goes dry (14:11), and like boulders which tumble down from a mountain or rocks which are worn away by water (14:18-19). When Job says in this context, "If a man die, shall he live again?" (14:14), his answer is emphatically "No!" (see verses 10, 12). However, he is not thinking of life after death in heaven or hell, but of living again on the earth in order to have an opportunity to defend his innocence in a court trial.

Summary of Job's Position
in the First Round of the Debate

When one arranges the ideas of Job in these early speeches, he finds the following points and emphases. First, my friends have failed to comfort me, or to show that all righteous people prosper and all wicked people suffer (6:14-30; 13:4-12).

Second, I am innocent of such great sins as the severity of my afflictions might lead one to believe (6:10, 24, 30; 10:7; 14:13-17), but I cannot prove it because God will not give me an opportunity to do so (9:2-12; 12:7-13:2; 13:23).

Third, God is arbitrary in his dealings with mankind (9:22; 10:14-15; 12:4, 6), which is illustrated, among other things, by the fact that he is making me, an innocent and blameless man, suffer without just cause (6:4; 7:20; 10:2-7; 13:23).

④ Fourth, I beg, yea challenge, God to meet me in a court trial so I can prove my innocence and that he has made me suffer without just cause (9:3, 15-16, 19-20, 32-35; 13:3, 15-16, 18-23; 14:13-17); but I fear that I will die without being given this opportunity, and if this happens I can never again return to this earth to defend my cause (7:8-10; 10:21-22; 14:7-17).

⑤ Fifth, I want to die because my suffering is greater than any man can bear (6:8-9; 7:13-19; 10:20-22; 14:13). Life is too short for one to have to suffer so severely (7:6-10; 14:1-6), and not be allowed to meet God in a court trial (9:25-26).

Now while some of these thoughts are contrary to the truth and out of harmony with God's will (see 40:8; 42:5-6), at least Job is making an honest attempt to grapple with the realities of life with which he is confronted, and to understand the nature of God and of man and of their relationship to one another in light of this.

Review   Questions

1. What do the following verses have to do with evaluating Job's statements in the first series of the debate, and in fact throughout all his speeches? Job 40:8; 42:5-6, 7-8. Discuss.

2. What three arguments does Job give in Job 6-7 to justify his right to complain? Discuss the validity of each argument.

3. Enumerate the seven illustrations Job gives to show his complaining about his suffering and his longing for death are justified by the severity of his afflictions. Job 6:1-13; 7:1-10.

4. What two illustrations does Job give to show that his friends have let him down in his hour of deepest need? Job 6:14-30.

5. What three charges or accusations does Job bring against God in his response to Bildad? Job 9-10. Evaluate each charge.

6. Discuss Job's point in Job 9:30-33. What kind of situation is envisioned here? Who is the "umpire" Job has in mind? Discuss.   *What does he mean by it?*

7. List Job's three points in his address to his friends in Job 12:1-13:19. Discuss each point.

8. What two points does Job make in his address to God in Job 13:20-14:22? Discuss each of these.

9. Discuss Job's question, "If a man die, shall he live again?" (Job 14:14), in its context. With what is Job concerned here? What is his answer to this question?

10. Enumerate the eight illustrations Job uses in the first round of the debate to describe the brevity of life. Job 7:6, 7, 9; 9:25-26; 14:2.

11. Summarize the five major points Job makes in the first round of the debate. Discuss each of these.

Lesson VI

THE PLEA OF "NOT GUILTY"
(Job 16-17, 19, 21, 23-24, 26-31)

"My foot has held fast to his steps;
I have kept his way and have not turned aside"
(Job 23:11)

"I hold fast my righteousness, and will not let it go;
my heart does not reproach me for any of my days"
(Job 27:6)

In the second and third rounds of the debate with his friends, on several issues Job simply repeats the views he had expressed in the first round. For example, he reiterates his innocence, reaffirms the incorrectness of his friends' position, declares that God acts arbitrarily in his dealings with man, challenges God to meet him in a court trial, and so forth. Only brief treatment of fundamental repetitions will be given in his lesson. At the same time, Job also opens new vistas of thought or expands significantly on some he had previously mentioned. These will call for somewhat fuller treatment here.

Job's Second Response to Eliphaz (Job 16-17)

This speech can be divided into two parts. First, Job reaffirms that his friends' position is wrong (16:1-5), and that God is making him suffer (16:6-16) although he is a righteous man (16:17). He says God has broken him asunder like a powerful warrior crushes a helpless foe in hand-to-hand combat (16:12, 14), and has pierced him through like an expert archer shoots arrows through a target or bull's eye (16:12-13).

(2) Second, Job prays that after his death the God he has always served and trusted (the God of his mind) will be his "witness" in a court trial against the God who is making him suffer (the God of his present experience), and will show one and all that Job is innocent and God has severely afflicted him without just cause. He prays that his blood, like Abel's (see Genesis 4:10), will cry out unto the God who always does right to bring to justice his murderer, God (16:18-21). He proposes this possibility of being vindicated because he is convinced that death is very near and that his friends will always believe he is a great sinner because his suffering is so great (16:22-17:7; 17:10-16). But he still believes there are righteous people on earth who will persevere in their righteousness in spite of the horrible way God has treated him (17:8-9) (16:18-17:16).

It should be emphasized that Job is not espousing the idea of two Gods in 16:18-21. Rather, he is struggling with what appears to him to be a contradiction in God's dealings with man. On the one hand, he has always believed God is just and thus causes all righteous people to prosper and all wicked people to suffer; but on the other hand, he is suffering terribly and yet is certain he has done nothing to deserve this. He is unwilling to abandon his faith in divine justice, and unable to deny his severe suffering; so he concludes that God is responsible for his affliction, and that God alone can vindicate him. Such a dilemma faces anyone whose openness to truth forces him to reexamine honestly his traditional beliefs.

Job's Second Response to Bildad (Job 19)

Job's speech here is strikingly similar to that in chapters 16-17, and also falls into two parts. First, he rebukes his friends for reproaching him and failing to

pity him (19:1-5, 21-22), and insists that God is afflicting
him (19:6, 8-20) without just cause (19:7) (19:1-22). God's
attack on Job is like an enemy army besieging a small
and helpless village (19:12).

(2) Second, Job yearns to be vindicated in two ways
(19:23-29). (a) He wishes his court case could be chiseled
deep into a rock so that when the God who is making
him suffer finally decides to appear, the record of Job's
character and behavior will expose him as unjust and
demonstrate Job's righteousness (19:23-24). (b) He feels
certain that the moral nature of the universe will some
day require that Job's "Redeemer" (that is, "Vindicator,"
"Blood Avenger," not "Savior from Sin"), the God in
whom he has always believed, appear on the earth to
defend Job against the God who is bringing all his
calamities upon him (19:25-27). Job closes by assuring his
friends that his afflictions are not divine punishment for
great sins he has committed (19:28-29). Note that Job
here is not desiring redemption from unforgiven sin as
the word "redeem" is often used in the New Testament,
but vindication of his righteousness, and demonstration of
God's unjust treatment of him. Verse 25 is not a predic-
tion of the coming of Christ, then. Some scholars think
Job believes God will vindicate him in heaven after his
death, but it is more likely that Job is seeking vindication at the place where the "murder" was committed,
that is, on earth. Job sees, in his mind's eye, God pro-
nouncing him innocent and the God who was making
him suffer, unjust.

Job's Second Response to Zophar (Job 21)

This entire chapter is an attempt to prove by the facts
of human life that God is arbitrary in his dealings with
man. Job begins by urging his friends to listen carefully
to his position (21:1-5). He avers that it is quite clear
from observing the lives and fates of men that there are
many wicked persons who live a long, prosperous life,
and are blessed as fully as they would be if they were

Wicked
do
prosper!

56

righteous (21:6-26). Finally, Job returns to his friends and challenges them to ask those who travel extensively about what happens to the wicked; they will say uniformly that many wicked prosper and are happy throughout life (21:27-34).

Job's Third Response to Eliphaz (Job 23-24)

The third round of the debate between Job and his friends contains problems. (1) Bildad's speech (chapter 25) is extremely short. (2) There is no speech of Zophar. (3) In certain places Job seems to defend the position of his friends against himself (especially in 24:18-20; 26:5-14; 27:13-23). A favorite solution is to rearrange certain portions of chapter 23-27, and to assign them to speakers other than those to whom they are attributed in the book as it now stands. The position taken in the present booklet is that it is preferable to leave the material as it now stands. Two considerations seem to support this. (a) The reason Bildad says so little and Zophar nothing is that they had already said all they could. This is indicated by the repetitions in their speeches, and by the statement in 32:3, 5 that Elihu became angry at the three friends because they said Job was wrong but found no answer to his arguments. (b) The passages in which Job seems to be taking the position of his friends may either be interpreted in a different way (26:5-14), or may be Job's quoting of certain arguments of his friends in order to refute them (24:18-20; 27:13-23).

Job's final reply to Eliphaz contains two paragraphs. First, he complains because God is making him suffer so severely (23:1-2). He longs to find God that he might meet him in a court trial, certain in his own mind that God would be forced to admit his innocence (23:3-7). Even though God has hidden himself so Job cannot find him anywhere, Job affirms that God's conscience is hurting him because he knows Job is righteous and does not deserve all this affliction (23:8-12). He is terrified of such a stubborn and unchanging God (23:13-17). This is his line of reasoning in chapter 23.

② Second, Job wonders why God does not right the wrongs in human life periodically by punishing the wicked and delivering the righteous (chapter 24). Instead, he turns a deaf ear to the suffering who cry out for help (24:12), and prolongs the life of the powerful and wicked rich (24:22). The friends' contention that the prosperity of the wicked is temporary (24:18-20) does not agree with the facts of life.

Job's Third Response to Bildad—Job's Final Speech (Job 26-31)

Job concludes the debate with a long speech in which he acknowledges God's power and wisdom but questions how he uses them, and then reasserts his innocence and dares God to meet him in a court trial.

First of all, Job affirms that God uses his unlimited power to do whatever he wishes, including crushing a helpless and innocent man (chapters 26-27). With great sarcasm, he chides his friends for failing him in his hour of deepest need (26:1-4). In a beautiful poem he points to undeniable evidences of the power of God in the created world, such as the suspension of earth in space, heavy clouds, the confining of the ocean waters within certain bounds, and the like (26:5-14). Yet he complains that God has used this power to prevent him from defending himself in a fair trial (27:2). He resolves that he will continue to be righteous no matter how God treats him (27:3-6), convinced that ultimately God will punish the wicked (27:7-10). In this way he will show he was right all along (27:11), and will demonstrate his friends' position was vain in affirming that all righteous people prosper (27:12-23; in verses 13-23 Job is quoting the "vain" position of his friends, which may be indicated simply by placing quotations marks around these verses or by inserting the word "saying" between verses 12 and 13).

Next, Job declares that wisdom is to be found with God alone, but asserts that God has used his wisdom to wreck Job's happy and prosperous life with suffering and affliction (chapters 28-30). (1) In another extremely beautiful poem (chapter 28; cf. 26:5-14), Job declares that whereas man is capable of mining all sorts of precious metals (28:1-11), he is incapable of finding wisdom by his own pursuits (28:12-22). God alone possesses wisdom, and the only way for man to possess it is for God to reveal it to him. God has done this from the very beginning by declaring to man that wisdom is to fear God and depart from evil (28:23-28). In the next three chapters, Job argues he has lived according to this principle, but still God has made him suffer. (2) Job yearns for "the months of old" (29:1), the "good ol' days" before all his calamities came upon him (chapter 29). That was a time when God blessed him with his friendship and his children were round about him (29:1-6), when he commanded the respect of his fellowmen like a "chief" and "king" in their midst (29:7-10, 21-25), and when he had the resources and energy to serve those who were in need (29:11-20). While these aspirations may cause one to empathize and sympathize with Job, the desires he expresses are very self-centered, and seem to cry out for redress. (3) In sharp contrast to his days of ease and good fortune (note "But now" in 30:1), Job turns to the bitter agonies of his present condition (chapter 30). Now the very lowest human beings mock him because they are certain God is punishing him for his great and many sins (30:1-15), he is constantly miserable because God has cast him into the mire (verse 19) and turned cruel to him (verse 21) (30:16-23), he stretches out his hand for someone to help and cries out for someone to comfort him, but to no avail (30:24-31).

Finally, Job states specific instances which illustrate his righteousness and challenges God to meet him in a court trial so he can vindicate himself (chapter 31). He affirms he is "not guilty" because: (a) he has not lusted after a virgin in his heart (31:1-4); (b) he has been

59

honest and sincere in dealing with his fellowmen (31:5-8); (c) he has not been enticed to or gone after another man's wife (31:9-12); (d) he has treated his servants with all dignity, and has listened lovingly and sympathetically to their complaints about their condition and his treatment of them (31:13-15); (e) he has provided generously for the needs of the disadvantaged — the poor, the widow, the orphan, and the naked (31:16-23); (f) he has not trusted in his wealth (31:24-25); (g) he has not worshiped creation (sun and moon) instead of the Creator 31:26-28); (h) he has not rejoiced over or prayed for the calamity of his enemy (31:29-30); (i) he has shown hospitality to travelers and strangers (31:31-32); (j) he has openly confessed his sins irrespective of jeers and negative reactions this might bring to him (31:33-34); and (k) he has paid a fair price for the land he has worked to raise crops for the sustenance of himself and his household (31:38-40).

It would be very difficult to find a higher ethical or moral standard than that assumed and expressed in this chapter. And yet there is something about Job's whole tone which rankles the mind. It smacks of the attitude of the Pharisee in Jesus' parable of the Pharisee and the publican (Luke 18:11-12). Indeed, Job feels that his "clean record" gives him the right to approach God "like a prince" (31:37), that is, an equal. Having thus stated his case, he signs the Affirmative, and challenges, yea even dares, God to sign the Negative (31:35). Job's religious and moral achievements were admittedly high, but the problem was that he prided himself in these achievements and was determined to force all men, and even God himself, to give him credit for them; and more than this, to praise him for them. Accordingly, Job's afflictions bring to the surface his real problem, which God was attempting to help him see and remove — self-righteousness, pride in his religious goodness.

As one looks back over Job's words in the second and third round of the debate, five main emphases stand out.

60

①
First, my friends have failed to comfort me, and their rigid view that all righteous people prosper and all wicked people suffer is incorrect (16:1-5, 20; 17:2, 4, 6, 10; 19:1-5, 21-22; 21:1-5, 27-28; 26:1-4; 27:5, 12-23; 30:26). ② Second, I want to die because I have no hope of getting better or of having an opportunity to defend myself against God (17:1, 7, 11-16; 23:13-17). Third, I am innocent ③ of any crime or sin which would warrant the terrible afflictions I am being forced to bear (16:18; 19:7; 23:6-7, 10-12; 27:3-6; 31). Fourth, God is arbitrary in the way he ④ deals with man; he is making me suffer without just cause (16:6-17; 19:6, 8-20; 21:7-34; 23—1-2, 13-17; 26:5-14; 27:2; 30:19-23). Fifth, I pray and even know that some ⑤ time after my death, the God whom I have always trusted and served will appear on earth in my behalf in a court trial and defend the fact that I did not deserve such severe suffering and that the God who is making me suffer did so unjustly (16:18-21; 19:23-27), since it seems quite clear the God who is making me suffer will not give me a chance to defend my case personally (23:3-12; 30:20).

See p. 505 for these same 5 things in different sequence

61

Review Questions

1. What fundamental charge does Job bring against God in his second response to Eliphaz and in his second response to Bildad? Job 16:6-17; 19:6-20. Have you ever felt this way about calamity or suffering in your own life? Discuss.

2. For what does Job yearn in his second response to Eliphaz? Job 16:18-21. Who is the "witness" in this passage? Discuss various views on this. *God*

3. In what two ways does Job yearn to be vindicated at the end of his second response to Bildad? Job 19:23-27. Who is the "redeemer" in verse 25. Compare him with the "umpire" in 9:33 and the "witness" in 16:19. Discuss.

4. What proof does Job give that God is arbitrary in his dealings with man in his second response to Zophar? Job 21:6-34. Do you agree with Job? Discuss.

5. In the third round of the debate, why is Bildad's speech so brief, why is there no speech of Zophar, and why does Job say several things which sound like the position of his friends? Job 32:3, 5. Discuss various attempts to solve this problem.

6. What two complaints does Job make against God in his third response to Eliphaz? Job 23-24. Discuss the validity of each complaint.

7. What two qualities of God does Job extol in his final speech? Job 26:5-14; 28. What criticism does Job have of God's use of these qualities?

8. For what three things did Job yearn in "the good ol' days"? Job 29. What three things upset him about his present situation? Job 30. Do you ever have similar feelings? Discuss.

9. List the eleven things Job enumerated to prove he was a righteous man. Job 31. Do you think the moral and religious standards lying behind this are commendable? Discuss. What is wrong with Job's defense here? Job 31:35-37. Is it possible for Christians in the modern world to be guilty of the same sin? Discuss.

10. Summarize the five main emphases of Job in the second and third rounds of the debate.

Elihu

Lesson VII

LET GOD BE GOD (Job 32-37)

"Behold, God is exalted in his power;
who is a teacher like him?" (Job 36:22)

Now for the first time in the book of Job one learns that someone else (and perhaps several other people) was present listening to the debate between Job and his friends. He was a young man named Elihu, a Buzite. He had not spoken because those who were engaging in the debate were quite a bit older than he (32:4). But now that the debate has come to an end, he can contain himself no longer. He is convinced that both sides have left several loose ends dangling, and that there is much more to be said. Two fundamental things motivate him to speak: (a) Job is righteous in his own eyes (32:1) and has justified himself rather than God (32:2); and (b) the three friends have declared Job to be wrong, but have found no answer to his arguments (32:3, 5) (32:1-5). Elihu demonstrates that insight and helpfulness do not depend on physical age, but on the personal sensitivity and concern of the individual.

Some scholars regard Elihu as a harsh, dull, uncreative, arrogant, angry young man, who does nothing more than talk a great deal, simply repeating the position of the friends. However, a careful study of his speeches indicates his whole attitude, approach, and viewpoint are quite different from that of Eliphaz, Bildad, and Zophar, and what he says begins to reach into Job's heart and deal with the problems he is facing. Viewed in this light, Elihu plays a very important role in the progress of Job's spiritual growth. When Job ended his last

64

speech with his challenge or dare to God to meet him in a court trial (31:35-37), he was in no mental or spiritual condition to listen to God even if he were to appear. Yet when God does appear in the whirlwind and speaks to Job, Job is very receptive (38:1-42:6). In between these two events, a great transformation must have taken place in Job's attitude and thinking. Elihu provides the explanation for this. He dealt with Job in such a skillful way as to prepare his heart to listen to God when God appeared. God, as it were, takes up where Elihu leaves off, and gently guides Job to repentance and newness of life. This explains why it is not necessary for God to evaluate Elihu at the end of the book as he does Job (40:8; 42:5-6) and his friends (42:7-8).

Elihu's speeches fall into six paragraphs according to content. It is true that introductions of Elihu occur in 32:6; 34:1; and 36:1; and Elihu's address to Job in 33:1 and 37:14, and to Job's three friends in 34:10 might be taken as beginnings of new sections. However, in this study the guideline will be content.

Elihu seeks to put Job at ease (Job 32:6-33:7)

The purpose of Job's friends had been to defeat Job in religious debate, to show that the long-standing view that all righteous people prosper and all wicked people suffer is correct. In contrast to this attitude, the first thing Elihu does to open Job's heart to listen to God is to assure Job he does not think he knows all the answers to life's puzzles, and that he is not interested in winning a debate. Three times he states his intention is but to give his "opinion" (32:6, 10, 17). He tells the friends that they have not answered Job's arguments (32:12; see verses 15-16), and states he will not reason with Job as they have done (32:14). Then he assures Job that he realizes he is but a man like Job is, constantly dependent on God's "spirit" or "breath" for life (33:4), "formed from a piece of clay" (33:6). He urges Job to stop him at any time and defend his position (33:5; see also verses

32-33), and pleads with him not to be afraid that he is trying to put him down or to put him under any kind of pressure (33:7). Elihu realizes the possibility of winning a debate only to lose a soul, and recognizes how much more important is the latter than the former.

God can speak to Man in more than one way (Job 33:8-33)

In order to make sure he correctly understands Job's position, Elihu quotes it in his own words: Job says, I am innocent, and yet God makes me suffer without just cause (33:9-11). Since Job does not stop Elihu, apparently Elihu is correct about this. To this Elihu responds that "God is greater than man" (33:12). Apparently he means that it is human to make someone's life miserable for no good reason, but if God does this he is no greater than man; and that God knows what is best for man and thus may have very good reasons for doing what he does which lie beyond man's finite comprehension; thus man is in no position to question God's activities.

Job also accused God of refusing to appear and speak with him to give him a chance to defend himself (33:13). Elihu replies that God may well have been speaking to Job all along, although in a way different from direct address, and Job has been talking so much himself that he has not heard God speak. He outlines in four steps one way in which God may deal with man to rid him of his "pride" (33:17). (1) He speaks to him in a "dream" or night "vision" while he is asleep, in order to terrify him and bring him to repent of his self-centeredness (33:14-18). In other words, first God tries a "gentle approach" to turn man from his pride. If this does not work, he must resort to sterner measures. (2) God chastens man with severe and continual illness so that he comes near death (33:19-22). Elihu seems to have Job's disease in mind here. (3) God provides "an angel, a mediator" to explain to the sufferer what is right or best for him, namely, to accept his suffering as God's means of helping him grow spiritually; and to intercede in behalf of the sufferer that God deliver him from death (33:23-25). Apparently Elihu is Job's angel-mediator here. (4) The sufferer prays to God, confessing his sin and asking forgiveness, and God accepts him; then he joyfully tells his fellowmen that even though he had sinned, God had been gracious to him and delivered him from death (33:26-30). This is precisely what Job does at the end of the book (see 42:5-8, 10-17).

God is not Arbitrary (Job 34)

Once again (as in 33:9-11), Elihu states his understandstanding of Job's basic position in order to make sure he is correctly representing him. Job says, I am innocent, and yet God is making me suffer without just cause (34:5-6); consequently, there is no profit in living a godly life (34:9). In this last observation Elihu places his finger on the real issue in the book of Job, namely, whether a human being will serve God faithfully and continually if there is no indication or promise of reward for so doing. In other words, will one serve God for unselfish motives, simply as a natural response of gratitude and appreciation for what God has done for him? (see 1:9). Again, Job does not interrupt Elihu, so apparently he agrees with Elihu's analysis of his point of view.

First (in 34:10-37), Elihu deals with the charge that God is unjust. He advances three arguments to demonstrate that this cannot be the case. (1) By definition, God must be just, for he is creator of all that is and consequently is in charge of everything and has absolute right to do whatever he pleases. The very fact that he sustains life on earth proves his genuine concern for all men (34:10-15). God's dealings with man may *appear* unjust to man at various times, but this does not make it so. (2) That all men die — kings, nobles, princes, rich, and poor — indicates God is in control of the world and governs without partiality to one above the other (34:17-20). (3) Men judge their fellows on the basis of limited knowledge, but God knows "all" his (that is, man's) steps" (34:21). Thus he blesses or curses man out of full knowledge and in order to accomplish what is best for him. In light of this,

"When he (that is, God) is quiet, who can condemn?
When he hides his face, who can behold him,
whether it be a nation or a man?" (34:29).

And who knows but what God may be blessing some "wicked" people because they repented and turned to God without the "righteous" (like Job, or his friends) knowing that they had done so? (34:31-33). Elihu, then, rebukes Job for condemning God's governance of the world and of the lives of individuals without possibly being able to know all the facts (34:35-37). In other words, Elihu reproves Job for his reaction to his suffering without attempting to discover or explain why Job was suffering in the first place.

Man must give an account to God, not God to man (Job 35)

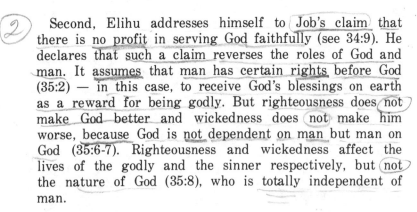

Second, Elihu addresses himself to Job's claim that there is no profit in serving God faithfully (see 34:9). He declares that such a claim reverses the roles of God and man. It assumes that man has certain rights before God (35:2) — in this case, to receive God's blessings on earth as a reward for being godly. But righteousness does not make God better and wickedness does not make him worse, because God is not dependent on man but man on God (35:6-7). Righteousness and wickedness affect the lives of the godly and the sinner respectively, but not the nature of God (35:8), who is totally independent of man.

It is characteristic of human beings to call on God for help when they are in trouble or oppressed, but to take his gifts for granted without thanking him when all is going well (35:9-11). Therefore, frequently he does not answer man's cries for help because they are petitioning him out of self-interest or "pride" (35:12-13). And certainly he will not answer a human subpoena like Job's (35:14-16), who complains because God will not appear and claims that if he should appear he could expose him "dead to rights" in a court trial without any difficulty (see 23:3-13; 31:35-37). It would be beneath God's dignity to answer the challenge of a proud and angry righteous man who thinks God should be proud of him and owes him something because he is righteous. The principle expressed here is powerfully illustrated by Jesus' teaching concerning a servant who had spent all day plowing and keeping sheep under the hot sun. When he comes in from the field in the evening, his master does not invite him to sit down with him at the table, but instructs him to prepare supper and serve it to him. And he does not thank the servant for this, because the servant is expected to do what the master commands. Likewise, if God's servants should do all he commands (and, of course, none does), they are still unworthy because they have done no more than their duty (Luke 17:7-10). Thus, it is wrong for Job or anyone else to expect God to bless them out of gratitude for their service to him.

God Teaches the Arrogant Humility by Suffering (Job 36:1-23).

Elihu declares that God is "perfect in knowledge" (36:4; see 37:16), and unexcelled as a "teacher" (36:22). It may appear to man that he is arbitrarily blessing the wicked and punishing the righteous, but this is because man's perspective is so limited. When the righteous are afflicted,

"then he (that is, God) declares to them their work
and their transgressions, that they are behaving
arrogantly" 36:9).

And they must turn away from their pride to serve him (36:10-11). As strange as it may seem to human logic,

"He (that is, God) delivers the afflicted by their
affliction,
and opens their ear by adversity" (36:15).

69

Thus Job must stop complaining and charging God with injustice because of his suffering, for this is sin; instead, he must see his suffering for what it is — God's gracious means of helping him overcome his pride (36:17-21). This calls to mind Paul's threefold prayer that God remove his "thorn in the flesh," not realizing at the time that this was the Lord's means of keeping him from being too elated (II Corinthians 12:7-10).

Man cannot comprehend God's ways (Job 36:24-37:24).

Job's complaints and accusations against God assumed that man is capable of thoroughly understanding God's ways, intentions, and purposes, but this is not true (36:26; 37:5, 23). Man cannot even comprehend God's works in nature, much less what he is doing in the lives of men and nations, especially on the spiritual level. He cannot fathom how God uses the spreading of the clouds, thunder, and lightning to judge peoples and to give abundant food (36:29-31), or the snow and rain of winter to prevent man from doing his normal work so that he may realize his dependence on God (37:6-7), or wind, ice, and clouds to correct sinners or to prepare the land for good crops or to manifest his love to man (37:9-13). If Job cannot explain how God causes lightning or cannot comprehend the balancings of the clouds or spread out the skies (37:15-18), certainly he is in no position to understand and evaluate God's works in the lives of men, especially suffering. And God will not accept those who pass judgment on his works as if he, the creator and ruler of the universe, did not know what he was doing and what was best for all concerned, those "who are wise in their own conceit" (37:24).

Summary of Elihu's Thought

Since it was Elihu who was able to prepare Job's mind to listen to God, it is important to understand his fundamental views. These may be summarized briefly under four headings.

1. I am just a man like you are, Job, made out of clay and constantly dependent on God for life (33:4-7). I do not claim to have all the answers to the problem of suffering or any other problem, but would like to state my "opinion" (32:6, 10, 17). Relax, and feel free to stop me, correct my misconceptions, and inject your own thoughts at any time (33:5, 7, 32-33).

2. Man cannot comprehend God's ways, and thus he is in no position to evaluate or to sit in judgment on them (33:12; 36:26, 29-31; 37:5-19), and certainly is out of place to challenge God to meet him in a court trial so he can prove he is innocent and God has made him suffer without just cause (35:14-16).

3. God is just, even though often he may appear unjust to man, who has only limited knowledge and perspective on life as a whole (34:10-37).

4. Job's problem is the basic problem of all men — pride or self-centeredness (33:17; 36:9; 37:24). And God speaks to him through suffering to humble him and to turn him back to a God-centered life (33:14-30; 35:9-13; 36:8-10, 15, 17-21).

With these thoughts expressed by one with a loving and sympathetic attitude, Elihu has broken through the defensive mechanisms Job had erected to stave off his antagonistic "friends." Now Job is in a proper frame of mind to listen to God. "Then the Lord answered Job out of the whirlwind" (38:1).

Review Questions

1. What was it about Job's position, and what was it about the position of Job's friends, that made Elihu feel he had to speak? Job. 32:1-5. Discuss.

2. State three things about Elihu's attitude and about his general approach to Job which made Job listen to what he had to say. Job 32:6, 10-17; 33:4-7, 31-32. What can the modern Christian learn from Elihu about the proper way to approach people in order to help them?

3. According to Elihu, what were the three main arguments of Job which needed to be challenged? Job 33:9-11; 34:5-6, 9. Do you agree with Elihu? Discuss each of these.

4. List *in order* the four steps which should occur when God is dealing with the pride of man. Job 33:14-30. Discuss.

5. What three arguments does Elihu give to show that God cannot be unjust? Job 34:10-30. Discuss each of these. Do you think each is a valid argument?

6. Is the nature of God affected by man's righteousness or wickedness? Job 35:6-8. Who is affected by these things? Why is it that frequently God does not answer the prayers of a "righteous" person? Job 35:9-16. In light of this, discuss the way one should feel about his service to God.

7. What important lesson may God be trying to teach the righteous by causing them to suffer? Job 36:8-9, 15, 17-21. Discuss. How does II Corinthians 12:7-10 shed light on this concept?

8. Elihu declares that man is in no position to evaluate or sit in judgment on God's ways in human life, includ-

ing suffering, because man cannot even comprehend what God is doing in the physical world. State at least four specific examples of God's working in nature which man cannot comprehend. Job 36:29-30; 37:5-13, 15-18. State four things God may be trying to accomplish through various natural phenomena. Job 36:31; 37:13.

9. Give a four point summary of Elihu's speeches. Discuss and evaluate each point.

Lesson VIII

GOD'S WAYS ARE PAST TRACING OUT
(Job 38-42)

"O the depth of the riches both of the wisdom and the knowledge of God! how unsearchable are his judgments, and his ways past tracing out! For who hath known the mind of the Lord? or who hath been his counselor? or who hath first given to him, and it shall be recompensed unto him again? For of him, and through him, and unto him, are all things. To him be the glory for ever. Amen." (Romans 11:33-36).

Throughout the course of the debate, Job had done and said everything he knew to persuade God to appear so he could talk to him face to face (see 9:16; 13:3, 18-19; 23:3-10; 31:35-37). He felt confident that if God would just give him a fair chance, he would fill his mouth with arguments (23:4) and God would have to admit Job did not deserve all the suffering he was having to endure (14:15-17). In this frame of mind, Job was in no condition to listen to God if and when he did appear. But with sympathetic understanding and insightful observations, Elihu began to open Job's mind to a new dimension of understanding. Thus God appears in the whirlwind.

But God does not come to Job to answer his questions by explaining the reasons why he was suffering, or to debate with him in a court case, or because his conscience finally hurt him so badly that he was ashamed not to appear. Job thought he deserved an explanation for God's behavior, a logical reason for his severe suffering. What he really needed was (1) a comprehension that

God is wiser and more powerful than any man could ever hope to imagine, and (2) a deeper faith in God as God. What he needed was not an answer to his questions, but an unwavering assurance that he could always depend on his Creator under all circumstances, which produces an intimate, personal, daily relationship with him. And this is precisely what God comes to give.

God begins both of his speeches (38:3; 40:7) by putting things back into their proper perspective. First of all, when he speaks to Job he is not speaking to a "worm" (see 25:6) or to an equal, a "prince" (see 31:37), but to a "man" whom he had created in his own image. Second, since he is God, it is his place to ask the questions and man's place to respond to them. Man is in no position to question God. God does not give an account of himself to man, but man to God.

A number of scholars view the book of Job from a humanistic point of view, and thus assume that God's speeches are in reality the position of the author of the book of Job, put into God's mouth to establish authority. Accordingly, some criticize the position expressed here as inferior to that found elsewhere in the book or as incorrect, and some argue that one or both of these speeches did not belong to the original book. The present writer believes God's viewpoint is correctly recorded here, and that the positions of the various speakers found elsewhere in the book must be evaluated in light of what God has to say.

God's First Speech — No Man can explain or control creation (Job 38:1-40:2)

Job had complained that God acts arbitrarily and unjustly in dealing with man. This assumes Job has at least as much knowledge of life and existence as God, if not more. Thus in God's first speech, he summons Job to explain why things are as they are in the physical world and/or to make them happen as they do. If he can demonstrate his wisdom and power in the more tangible, less complicated physical realm, then he can show the likelihood that he is able to evaluate the less tangible, more complicated spiritual realm correctly. In order to convey this thought. God uses examples of inanimate creation, beasts, and birds.

1. Examples of Inanimate Creation (Job 38:1-38). God calls on eight examples from the sphere of non-animal life to emphasize his point. Note how he asks, "*Who* did this or that?", "*Have you* done this or that?", "*Can you* do this or that?", and intersperses these with statements like, "Tell me, if you have understanding" (38:4), "Surely you know!" (38:5), "Declare, if you know all this" (38:18), and

"You know. for you were born then,
    and the number of your days is great!" (38:21).

God's eight examples cover a wide range of concerns relating to the past, the present, and the future. Do you know how it all started? Do you know where everything is in the universe? Can you keep everything running from now on? (a) Where were you (Job) when I created the world, building it like a carpenter builds a house? (38:4-7). (b) Who was it that made the oceans and seas of the earth such that they would come up on the land so far and no farther? (38:8-11). (c) Have you ever caused the sun to rise so that the colorless black and white of night gives way to the brilliant colors of life apparent in the bright sunlight? (38:12-15). (d) Do you know where the underground springs are which constantly replenish the water supply of the oceans and seas so that they never run dry, or where the gates of death are, through whom the deceased pass into eternity? (38:16-18).

(e) Where are light and darkness and snow and hail and the east wind kept stored up until they are needed to accomplish God's purpose on earth? (38:19-24). Note here that "the treasures of the snow" of the KJV (38:22) are not "treasures which come out of the snow," but "treasuries" (ASV) or "storehouses" (RSV; see the NEB) "out of which the snow comes," as it is stored up there (the language, of course, is figurative). Note also that one purpose for which God might use one or more of these elements is to cripple or totally prevent human intentions to cause trouble or to engage in war (38:23). (f) Who causes it to rain where men do not live so that vegetation can grow there and provide food for animals and birds, and whence comes dew, ice, and hoarfrost to freeze over lakes, ponds, and streams? (38:25-30). (g) Can you keep the constellations like the Pleiades, the Orion, the Mazzaroth, and the Bear (Ursa Major — the Big Dipper) in the orbits, and cause them to be at their proper places in the sky during the various seasons of the year, so that they can benefit the earth as they are intended? (38:31-33). (h) Can you command the clouds so they will appear to act like wise men and pour out rain on the earth at the proper time, like one pours water out of a waterskin? (38:34-38).

It is noteworthy that both Job (9:4-12; 26:5-14) and his friends (5:8-10; 11:7-12; 22:12-14) speak of God's power and wisdom manifested in creation. But Paul declares that if one takes this seriously it will cause him to honor God as God and give him thanks (Romans 1:20-21), which neither Job nor his friends did. Evidently, then, their allusions to God's power and wisdom reflected in the universe do not indicate a real application of a professed belief in these things to their daily practical religious thinking, but are merely abstract dogmas which they feel they can use to defend their respective intellectual positions.

2. Examples of Beasts (Job 38:39-40; 39:1-12, 19-25). Further, God selects five examples of beasts to demonstrate the incomprehensibility of his wisdom and power by man. (a) Can you (Job) hunt your food like the lion? (38:39-40). The point is that the reason the lion obtains his food as he does and man as he does is that God has made each to do so in his own way. Thus man cannot

secure his food as does a lion. He is totally dependent on a different means of doing so just because God made him this way. (b) Do you know when the mountain goats give birth to their young? Are you there to guard the young as they grow to maturity and leave their dens to live their own adult lives? (39:1-4). The point is that it is extremely difficult for human beings to observe the activities of mountain goats, because they are so wary of men and strive to stay away from them. But without any human aid, they are able to do quite well. How is this? (c) Who has given the wild ass its peculiar characteristics of resisting attempts to be tamed, of living in the steppe and the salt land, and of pasturing in the mountains? (39:5-8). (d) Can you tame the wild ox and use him for domestic work like plowing or threshing grain? (39:9-12). (e) Are you the one who gave the horse just the right temperament and ability to suit him for use by man in military conflict? Whence came the strength, the ability to leap, the absence of the fear of danger, and the anxiety to go forth to the battle, all woven together so skilfully and proportionately into one animal? (39:19-25). These peculiar attributes of a few select animals, along with thousands of others which might have been chosen, point to one whose wisdom and power far transcends anything man could possibly comprehend.

3. Examples of Birds (Job 38:41; 39:13-18, 26-30). God also appeals to three examples of birds to emphasize his inscrutable power and wisdom. (a) Who sees to it that the raven has ample prey to secure food for itself and its young? (38:41). (b) It might appear to human wisdom that the ostrich is stupid, because she lays her eggs on the ground and often forgets where she laid them. Yet ostriches survive, and when grown are able to outrun pursuing horses carrying hunters (39:13-18). This is but another manifestation of God's wisdom which lies beyond man's comprehension. (c) Are you (Job) the one who gave the falcon the wisdom to migrate at the proper time each year, or who taught the eagle to build its nest on high rocky areas for safety and to be able to see its

prey at a great distance and to be a scavenger? (39:26-30). Since you have found fault with God's ways because of your affliction, show your wisdom by answering these simpler questions pertaining to the physical realm (40:2).

Job's Reply to God's First Speech—Silence (Job 40:3-5).

At one point during the debate, Job had boasted that if God would appear and give him a chance to defend himself, he would fill his mouth with arguments (23:4). But when God does appear and begins asking Job about various phenomena in the world about him, Job has nothing to say. He admits that God's power and wisdom are far beyond his ability to understand or explain, and thus he had spoken out of turn. But God does not want Job's silence. He wants Job. Thus he continues in a second speech.

God's Second Speech—Man is unable to run the universe (Job 40:6-41:34).

In his second speech, God first states an important lesson Job needs to learn, then gives two illustrations from among the creatures he made to support it.

1. The Lesson (40:6-14). God begins by rebuking Job for arguing God is wrong and condemning God that he (Job) might be justified (40:8). Thus Job's basic sin is daring to pass judgment on his Creator and the ruler and sustainer of the universe. God invites Job to come upon his throne and show him how to deal with one who is "proud" (40:10-13). After he does this successfully, God will grant him that he is right and God is wrong in the way he deals with men (40:14), especially a proud man like Job.

2. The First Illustration—the Hippopotamus (40:15-24). God challenges Job to capture (40:24) "Behemoth," usually thought to be the hippopotamus. He emphasizes

that the hippopotamus is much stronger than man (40:16), yet God made this animal (40:15, 19). But if Job is unable to prevail against the hippopotamus, surely he is no match for God, who created the hippopotamus.

3. The Second Illustration—the Crocodile (chapter 41). Similarly God suggests that Job "go fishing" (41:1-2) for "Leviathan," perhaps the crocodile, then engage him in hand-to-hand combat.

"Lay hands on him; think of the battle;
  you will not do it again! (41:8)

But if Job cannot successfully defeat the crocodile in a physical dual, surely there is no way for him to defeat the Creator of the crocodile in a spiritual battle (41:10-11). If the creature is too strong for Job (41:12, 22), the Creator must be as well.

[handwritten margin note: What about vss 18-21? Sounds more like a fire breathing dragon form.]

Job's Reply to God's Second Speech—Repentance (Job 42:1-6)

With this, God has penetrated to the very heart of Job, and Job admits God can do anything he desires without asking man or being answerable to human complaints (42:2). He confesses that he had tried to cope with matters and reason about situations which lie beyond man's sphere of knowledge or power (42:3). This is because his faith in God had been a "hand-me-down" faith, not one which grows out of personal experience (42:5). Therefore, he repents (42:6), which in the context of the book of Job must mean he denounced his former insistence that God owed him something for his righteousness, that God had singled him out arbitrarily to make him suffer without just cause, and that the world could certainly be governed in a much better way.

God's Reconciliation of Job and his Friends (Job 42:7-17)

After Job repents, God appears to Eliphaz and tells him he and his friends deserve punishment because they not

had ~~been~~ spoken right concerning him as Job had (42:7, 8). This cannot mean Job was all right and his friends were all wrong, but that Job was closer to the truth than they. This includes the fact that Job honestly struggled with his problem and ultimately repented, whereas his friends did nothing more than "parrot" long-held beliefs, and closed their eyes to the reality which lay before them. Job rightly saw that from man's perspective God appears to be unjust in dealing with men and nations, but he did not hold open the possibility that man might not be in a position to view all things in proper perspective. God instructs Job's friends to offer sacrifices and to have Job pray for them in order that he not punish them. They do what God commands, and he accepts Job's prayer (42:8-9).

Then God gives Job twice as much as he had before. His brothers and sisters come to him and sympathize with him and comfort him "for all the evil that the Lord had brought upon him" (42:11). Job lives another 140 years (42:10-17). It would be a mistake to interpret these divine blessings as a "reward" for Job's goodness or repentance. Because Job had learned firsthand to trust in God as Creator and sustainer of the universe, and to do without his health and wealth, now God could trust him with it. Job did not expect this restoration of his fortunes or think God owed it to him, but God gave it to him nevertheless. What a great lesson Job had learned!

Review Questions

1. How does God begin both of his speeches to Job? Job 38:3; 40:7. What two important truths can one learn from this? Discuss.

2. What fundamental point is God trying to communicate to Job in his first speech? Job 38:1-40:2.

3. List the eight examples drawn from *non-animal* inanimate creation which God selects to show Job he has power and wisdom far beyond any man's comprehension. Job 38:1-38. Discuss each of these. Give special attention to the reference to the snow in verse 22.

4. Name the five examples of beasts which God uses to emphasize the inscrutability of his wisdom and power. Job 38:39-40; 39:1-12, 19-25. Discuss each of these.

5. Enumerate the three examples of birds God chooses to demonstrate his incomprehensibility. Job 38:41; 39:13-18, 26-310. Discuss each of these.

6. How does Job respond to God's first speech? Job 40:4-5. Why is a second speech necessary?

7. In God's second speech, how does God show Job once and for all that man is in no position to sit in judgment on God's dealings with men and nations? Job 40:8, 10-13. Discuss.

8. With what two of his creatures does God invite Job to enter into battle? Job 40:15, 24; 41:1-2, 8. What point is God making in issuing these challenges? Job 41:10-11. What important lesson can the modern Christian learn from this?

9. What is Job's response to God's second speech? Job 42:2-3, 5-6. What is probably included in his repen-

tance? Discuss in light of what Job had said during the course of the debate.

10. How does God deal with Job's friends after Job repents? Job 42:7-9. How does he deal with Job? Job 42:10-17. Do you think God is rewarding Job for being more correct than his friends, and for repenting after he heard what God had to say? Discuss.

Lesson IX

BASIC CHARACTERISTICS OF GOD AND MAN

"Many are the plans in the mind of a man, but it is the purpose of the Lord that will be established" (Proverbs 19:21).

Lessons IX-XII of this booklet deal with certain major teachings in the book of *Proverbs*. The biblical book of *Proverbs* consists primarily of disconnected proverbs, each dealing with a different subject. Therefore, it is impossible to go through this book in a logical way as in the case of *Job*. Rather, it is necessary to arrange the proverbs by similarity of subject matter. This admittedly has its disadvantages, as it is impossible to be exhaustive; and there is often difference of opinion as to the meaning of a given proverb. It is purposed that in this volume some of the main themes may be emphasized, and that the reader will study further on his own and classify the various proverbs according to subject matter.

Authorship, Composition, and Original Audience of the Book of Proverbs

Before the book of Proverbs existed in its present form, Solomon and other wise men spoke proverbs to various audiences on various occasions, probably ordinarily to pupils in a type of classroom situation, and in time different smaller collections of proverbs were made. Several things show that such smaller collections existed at one time. (1) There are several headings or superscriptions in the book of *Proverbs*, attributing various groups of proverbs to different writers (1:1, 10:1; 25:1—Solomon [see 1 Kings 4:29-34]; 22:17; 24:23—the wise men; 30:1—Agur; 31:1—Lemuel). (2) Certain unique kinds of proverbs are sometimes grouped together. For example, Proverbs 5-7 do not contain isolated proverbs for the most part, but are lengthy, coherent, logical poetic orations warning a young man of the dangers of going to the prostitute. Proverbs 30:18-31 contains numerical proverbs each consisting of four items. Proverbs 31:10-31 is the famous description of the good wife. (3) Several proverbs appear twice in the present book of Proverbs. For example, 14:12=16:25; 18:8=26:22; 19:24=26:15; 20:16=27:13; 21:9=25:24; 22:3=27:12. (4) Proverbs 22:17-24:22 is strikingly similar to the Egyptian Wisdom of Amen-em-opet (see Lesson I).

The overall thrust of the book of *Proverbs* suggests the proverbs contained therein were originally intended for young men preparing for positions of leadership in the Israelite government, although the applications of the truths taught therein are much broader than this. Only middle or upper class young men could afford most of the follies condemned in this book. It is logical to believe they had the time necessary to spend with the wise men. The social background and philosophical outlook presupposed in most proverbs points to the middle and upper class.

The main emphasis in this lesson concerns the teaching of the book of Proverbs on basic characteristics of God and man.

Characteristics of God

The book of Proverbs teaches that God is creator of heaven and earth and all that is within them (3:19-20). He is the maker of both rich and poor (22:2). That his creatures have the ability to hear and see is due to the fact that he made the ear and the eye (20:12; see Exodus 4:11). There is a very strong emphasis in this book on the fact that God created the world by "wisdom." Personified wisdom declares that God created her first of all (8:22-26), and then she was his constant companion in the creation of everything else. She says:

"When he established the heavens, I was there,
when he drew a circle on the face of the deep,
when he made firm the skies above,
when he established the fountains of the deep,
when he assigned to the sea its limit,
so that the waters might not transgress his command,
when he marked out the foundations of the earth,
then I was beside him, like a master workman;
and I was daily his delight,
rejoicing before him always,
rejoicing in his inhabited world
and delighting in the sons of men" (8:27-31).

God continually sustains and upholds the world he has created, carrying out his purposes (16:1, 4, 9, 33; 19:21; 20:24; 21:1, 30, 31). He scrutinizes man's motives and actions from the perspective of his infinite wisdom and matchless love.

"The crucible is for silver, and the furnace is for gold, and the Lord tries hearts" (17:3; see also 16:2; 21:2).

"The eyes of the Lord are in every place, keeping watch on the evil and the good" (15:3; see also 5:21; 15:11).

In light of this, he renders to each person what is best under the circumstances (3:33-34; 10:3, 29; 12:2; 16:7; 25:21-22; 29:26). He is especially concerned about the helpless, the needy, the widow, and the orphan (14:31; 15:25; 22:22-23).

While God does want sacrifice and prayer as acts of worship to him, he is more concerned that the one who approaches him in public worship be faithful to him and just and righteous in his dealings with his fellowmen.

"The sacrifice of the wicked is an abomination to the Lord,

but the prayer of the upright is his delight"
(15:8; see 21:3, 27).

Because God is good and because he wants what is
best for man, there are several things which he "hates"
because they are opposed to his very nature and destroy
man. A very famous passage says:

"There are six things which *the Lord hates,*
seven which are *an abomination to him:*
haughty eyes, a lying tongue,
and hands that shed innocent blood,
a heart that devises wicked plans,
feet that make haste to run to evil,
a false witness who breathes out lies,
and a man who sows discord among brothers"

(6:16-19).

In essence, the sins listed here which the Lord hates are
pride, lying, violence, injustice, slander, and sowing discord. A number of passages in the book of Proverbs
state that one human activity or another "is an abomination to the Lord." These include: (a) the prayer of one
who is disobedient to God (28:9); (b) arrogance or pride
(16:5); (c) men of perverse mind and action (3:32; 11:20;
15:26); (d) the sacrifice of a wicked person, especially
when he brings it with evil intent (21:27); (e) unjust
business practices (11:1; 20:20); (f) lying (12:22); and
(g) one who justifies the wicked and condemns the
righteous (17:15).

Characteristics of Man

The book of Proverbs emphasizes certain basic truths
about the nature of man. He is a creature made by God
(22:2), and thus is incapable of understanding God's ways
(30:2-4). Man's basic problem is pride. He is not willing
to admit that he is not in control of the universe, of life
on earth, and of his own actions and destiny. Accordingly, the book of Proverbs has a great deal to say about
the sin of pride.

87

"When pride comes, then comes disgrace;
but with the humble is wisdom" (11:2).
"Pride goes before destruction,
and a haughty spirit before a fall" (16:18).
"Haughty eyes and a proud heart,
the lamp of the wicked, are sin" (21:4).
"Do you see a man who is wise in his own eyes?
There is more hope for a fool than for him" (26:12).

Whereas the speech and actions of man are of great concern and serve to indicate one's real nature, the motives and intentions of the heart are of utmost importance. Thus the wise man urges his student:

"Keep your heart with all vigilance;
for from it flow the springs of life" (4:23).

That which one genuinely and diligently seeks will motivate his speech and actions, and ultimately will reveal the kind of person he is and determine his lifestyle.

"He who diligently seeks good seeks favor,
but evil comes to him who searches for it" (11:27).

See also 11:23; 21:8, 10; 22:11.

There are certain things which are true of all men, things which may be regarded as "universal characteristics" of man.

1. It is typical of most men at least to pretend to be something they are not.

"Many a man proclaims his own loyalty,
but a faithful man who can find?" (20:6).

2. Each man thinks he is right, although he may be in error or on the wrong course.

"There is a way which seems right to a man,
but its end is the way to death" (14:12, 16:25).
"Every way of a man is right in his own eyes,
but the Lord weighs the heart" (21:2; see 16:2).

3. All human beings are sinners and in need of God's grace.

"Who can say, 'I have made my heart clean;
I am pure from my sin'?" (20:9).

4. The future is not in man's hands, but in God's.

"Do not boast about tomorrow,
for you do not know what a day may bring forth"
(27:1; see James 4:13-17).

5. Man has an insatiable desire to know more and to *Eccles.!* possess more. He is never satisfied.

"Sheol and Abaddon are never satisfied,
and never satisfied are the eyes of man" (27:20).

6. When all is said and done, each person must rejoice or mourn for himself alone. When a man loses his wife in death, many may weep and sympathize, but none can feel the emptiness he experiences. Or when someone is successful, many may call or write to congratulate him, but he alone is able to feel the deep sense of satisfaction resulting from the great amount of time and effort he has expended to attain this achievement. In other words, there are some things too private and personal to share with any other human being.

"The heart knows its own bitterness,
and no stranger shares its joy" (14:10).

"Even in laughter the heart is sad, *We have a way of faking it* and the end of joy is grief" (14:13).

7. Good news makes a person happy.

"Like cold water to a thirsty soul,
so is good news from a far country"
(25:25; see 15:30). *The light of the eyes rejoices the heart, and good news refreshes the bones.*

8. Anxiety or worry (a pessimistic attitude) tears a man down and makes him gloomy and dejected. Conversely, happiness and cheerfulness (an optimistic outlook) builds him up and makes life worth living.

"Anxiety in a man's heart weighs him down,
but a good word makes him glad" (12:25).

"A cheerful heart is a good medicine,
but a downcast spirit dries up the bones" (17:22;
see 18:14).

9. A good, faithful, and godly friend improves a man's character and makes him a better than he would have been without him.

"Iron sharpens iron,
and one man sharpens another" (27:17).

Review Questions

1. Relate the process by which the book of Proverbs ~~p 84 #2~~ came into being in light of the biblical evidence. Give four arguments which indicate smaller collections of proverbs existed prior to the present book, which were incorporated into and came to make up the book. Discuss.

2. Name four authors or groups of authors whose proverbs appear in the book of Proverbs. Proverbs 1:1; 10:1; 25:1; I Kings 4:29-34; Proverbs 22:17; 24:23; 30:1; 31:1. *[handwritten: Solomon, wise men, Agur, Sol., Lemuel (p 86)]*

3. For whom were the proverbs now found in the book of Proverbs originally intended? Give three arguments which support this view. *[handwritten annotations throughout]*

[handwritten: P 85 1. Only middle or upper class, could afford the follies condemned in the book. 2. It is logical to think they had the time to spend w/the wise men. 3. The social background + philosophical outlook pre-]

4. State three specific things the book of Proverbs teaches concerning God as Creator. Proverbs 3:19-20; 22:2; 20:12. What role did "wisdom" play in creation? 8:22-36. Discuss. *[handwritten: p85-86 ... supposed in most proverbs points to middle + upper classes.]*

5. Enumerate some of the ways God works in his world and among men, according to the book of Proverbs. Proverbs 21:1, 30; 17:3; 3:33-34; 15:25. Discuss each of these.

6. List seven things that are an "abomination" to the Lord other than those things mentioned in Proverbs 6:16-19. Proverbs 28:9; 16:5; 11:20; 21:27; 11:1; 12:22; 17:15. Discuss each of these, and make practical applications for the modern Christian. *[handwritten: p87, 1-7]*

7. According to the book of Proverbs, what is man's basic problem? Proverbs 21:4; 26:12. What is of utmost importance in man's daily living? Proverbs 4:23. Discuss these two subjects. *[handwritten: -p87 @]*

[handwritten at bottom: p 88 @ ... motives + intentions of the heart. What one genuinely + diligently seeks will motivate his speech + actions, + ultimately will reveal the kind of person he is + determine his lifestyle.]

91

p88-90

8. Name nine "universal characteristics" of man depicted in the book of Proverbs. Proverbs 20:6; 14:12; 20:9; 27:1, 20; 14:10; 25:25; 12:25; 27:17. Discuss each of these in light of your own experience. Are there other universal characteristics of man which occur in the book of Proverbs that are not mentioned in this lesson? Let each member of the class give input on this matter.

Lesson X

the wise　　*the foolish*

WISDOM AND FOLLY, RICHES AND POVERTY, WORK AND LAZINESS

"He who trusts in his riches will wither,
but the righteous will flourish like a green leaf"
Proverbs 11:28)

The book of Proverbs abounds in contrasts (antithetic parallelism). Among the various contrasts which occur, the most prominent are those between wisdom and folly, riches and poverty, and work and laziness. Furthermore, these major issues of human life are so interrelated that they are closely intertwined throughout the book of Proverbs.

The Wise and the Foolish

There are many sharp distinctions between the wise and the foolish which are pointed out in the book of Proverbs. As attention is called to some of these, the definition of "wisdom" as "fearing God and departing from evil" suggested in Lesson II should be kept in mind.

1. The fool despises wisdom and instruction (1:7; 12:15; 28:26), whereas the wise man welcomes instruction and advice from godly friends and teachers (15:5, 14; 18:15). Thus he who would be a wise person is instructed:

"Listen to advice and accept instruction,
that you may gain wisdom for the future" (19:20).

93

"He whose ear heeds wholesome admonition
will abide among the wise.
He who ignores instruction despises himself,
but he who heeds admonition gains understanding"
(15:31-32).

2. The fool is quick to speak and express his opinion
without having thought through what he is saying, while
the wise takes time to study and meditate on a matter
and even then is slow to speak.

"A prudent man conceals his knowledge,
but fools proclaim their folly" (12:23).

"A fool takes no pleasure in understanding,
but only in expressing his opinion" (18:2)

"If one answers before he hears,
it is his folly and shame" (18:13).

See also 10:19; 13:3; 21:23.

3. The fool retaliates immediately and loses his self-
control, but one who is wise is slow to anger and
remains calm.

"A man of quick temper acts foolishly,
but a man of discretion is patient" (14:17).

"He who restrains his words has knowledge,
and he who has a cool spirit is a man of understanding.
Even a fool who keeps silent is considered wise;
when he closes his lips, he is deemed intelligent"
(17:27-28).

"A fool gives full vent to his anger,
but a wise man quietly holds it back" (29:11).

"He who is slow to anger is better than the mighty,
and he who rules his spirit than he who takes a city"
(16:32).

See further 12:16; 14:16; 19:11; 25:28; 29:9; James 1:19-20.

4. A fool repeats the same sins which hurt him, then
blames God for the affliction he has brought on himself.

6. a fool's lips bring strife,
and his mouth invites a
flogging.

7. A fool's mouth is his ruin
and his lips are a snare to
himself.

WISDOM AND FOLLY, RICHES AND POVERTY, WORK AND LAZINESS

"Like a dog that returns to his vomit
is a fool that repeats his folly"
(26:11; see II Peter 2:20-22).

"When a man's folly brings his way to ruin,
his heart rages against the Lord" (19:3). *blames God!*

(4b) See also 18:6-7. By way of contrast, a wise man flees
from evil. The wise man instructs his son:
"Do not enter the path of the wicked,
and do not walk in the way of evil men.
Avoid it; do not go on it;
turn away from it and pass on.
For they cannot sleep unless they have done wrong;
they are robbed of sleep unless they have made someone stumble.
For they eat the bread of wickedness and drink
the wine of violence.
But the path of the righteous is like the light of dawn,
which shines brighter and brighter until full day.
The way of the wicked is like deep darkness;
they do not know over what they stumble" (4:14-19).

5. The fool enjoys wickedness, whereas the wise takes
pleasure in righteousness.

"It is like sport to a fool to do wrong,
but wise conduct is pleasure to a man of
understanding" (10:23).

6. A fool has aspirations *for unattainable goals* far beyond his abilities and is
easily distracted from concentration on meaningful and
attainable goals, while a wise man is realistic and suits
his interests to his capabilities.

"A man of understanding sets his face toward wisdom,
but the eyes of a fool are on the ends of the earth"
(17:24)

7. The fool loves to cause strife, but the wise is quick
to forgive and strives to settle a dispute promptly.

"It is an honor for a man to keep aloof from strife;
but every fool will be quarreling" (20:3).

"Hatred stirs up strife,
but love covers all offenses" (10:12; see I Peter 4:8).

Also compare 10:18; I Corinthians 13:7; James 5:20.

The Rich and the Poor

One's attitude toward wealth plays a very important role in his ability or lack of ability to serve God acceptably. The book of Proverbs contains a great deal of teaching on this very prevalent human problem.

1. *Reasons for Wealth and Poverty.* Wealth may come in a wide variety of ways. One may inherit riches from his forebears (19:14). The wicked often gain wealth by violence or unjust means, but ultimately it will not profit him.

"Treasures gained by wickedness do not profit,
but righteousness delivers from death" (10:2).

"The getting of treasures by a lying tongue
is a fleeting vapor and a snare of death" (21:6).

See also 11:16; 28:6. Some amass riches by hard work.

"A slack hand causes poverty,
but the hand of the diligent makes rich" (10:4).

See further 12:11; 13:4; 14:23; 21:5. And God often blesses the righteous with wealth.

"The reward for humility and the fear of the Lord
is riches and honor and life" (22:4).

Also see 3:9-10, 16; 10:22; 15:6. Poverty also may be due to several different things. One may become poor through the injustice of others toward him.

"The fallow ground of the poor yields much food,
but it is swept away through injustice"
(13:23).

Or poverty may be the result of divine punishment.

"Misfortune pursues sinners,
but prosperity rewards the righteous"
(13:21; see also 22:16).

Further, it may come because one refuses to follow
sound advice.

"Poverty and disgrace come to him who ignores
instruction,
but he who heeds reproof is honored" (13:18).

Following worthless pursuits or laziness rather than diligent work leads to poverty.

"He who tills his land will have plenty of bread,
but he who follows worthless pursuits will have
plenty of poverty" (28:19).

Using an object lesson, the wise man says:

"I passed by the field of a sluggard,
by the vineyard of a man without sense;
and lo, it was all overgrown with thorns;
the ground was covered with nettles,
and its stone wall was broken down.
Then I saw and considered it;
I looked and received instruction.
A little sleep, a little slumber,
a little folding of the hands to rest,
and poverty will come upon you like a robber,
and want like an armed man"
(24:30-34; see also 6:6-11).

Gluttony and drunkenness bring one to poverty.

"Be not among winebibbers,
or among gluttonous eaters of meat;
for the drunkard and the glutton will come to poverty,
and drowsiness will clothe a man with rags"
(23:20-21).

2. *Attitudes toward wealth.* Riches are good or evil
depending on how the rich man views them.

"One man gives freely, yet grows all the richer,

another withholds what he should give, and only
suffers want.
A liberal man will be enriched,
and one who waters will himself be watered"
(11:24-25).

Wealth can be very helpful in serving God if he who has
possessions loves the Lord and is willing and ready to
help those who are in need. Many work to have to hold.
Paul declares that the Christian must work to have to
give (Ephesians 4:28). Actually there are powerful
temptations to forsake God both in riches and in poverty.
The wise man Agur utters this prayer to the Lord:

"Two things I ask of thee;
deny them not to me before I die:
Remove far from me falsehood and lying;
give me neither poverty nor riches:
feed me with the food that is needful for me,
lest I be full, and deny thee,
and say, 'Who is the Lord?'
or lest I be poor, and steal,
and profane the name of my God" (30:7-9).

The time and energies of one whose life is committed to
God will not be consumed in the pursuit of wealth.
Riches which will prove to be stable and enduring are
those which come slowly and not quickly, so that he who
possesses them appreciates the fact that they come from
God, that he can live without them, and that his faith is
not in them.

"Wealth hastily gotten will dwindle,
but he who gathers little by little will increase
it" (13:11).

"A miserly man hastens after wealth,
and does not know that want will come upon
him" (28:22).

See also 20:21; 28:20. It is not riches which turn one
away from God, but the trust in riches.

"He who trusts in his riches will wither,

v 4 Do not toil to acquire wealth; be wise enough to desist.
v 5 When your eyes light upon it, it is gone; for suddenly it takes to
itself wings, flying like an eagle toward heaven.

WISDOM AND FOLLY, RICHES AND POVERTY, WORK AND LAZINESS

but the righteous will flourish like a green leaf"
(11:28).

See further 23:4-5. Many things in life are of much
greater value and importance than wealth. One is lips
which speak knowledge.

"There is gold, and abundance of costly stones;
but the lips of knowledge are a precious jewel"
A word fitly spoken is like apples of gold in a setting of silver. (20:15).
Also see 25:11. A good reputation is worth much more
than great wealth.

"A good name is to be chosen rather than great riches,
and favor is better than silver or gold" (22:1).

There is no comparison between the value of riches and
righteousness. *Riches do not profit in the day of wrath, but
righteousness delivers from death.*
"Better is little with righteousness
than great revenues with injustice" (16:8).

See also 11:4; 15:16; 16:19; 19:1, 22; 28:6. Wisdom, that
is, fearing God and departing from evil, is far more
important to human life than great wealth.

"Happy is the man who finds wisdom,
and the man who gets understanding,
for the gain from it is better than gain from silver
and its profit better than gold.
She is more precious than jewels,
and nothing you desire can compare with her"
(3:13-15).
See further 2:1-5.

3. *Responsibilities of the rich toward the poor.* Since
God's immeasurable wealth alone can enable any man to
be rich, and since God has blessed some with wealth, it
is the natural responsibility of the rich who are godlike
to help the poor. After all, God is creator of both rich
and poor (22:2), and so to oppress or neglect the poor is
to insult the creator himself.

"He who oppresses a poor man insults his Maker,
but he who is kind to the needy honors him" (14:31).

99

It is unfortunate that usually people go out of their way to try to befriend the wealthy, but avoid association with the poor.

> "Wealth brings many new friends,
> but a poor man is deserted by his friend . . .
> Many seek the favor of a generous man,
> and every one is a friend to a man who gives gifts.
> All a poor man's brothers hate him;
> how much more do his friends go far from him!
> He pursues them with words, but does not have
> them" (19:4, 6-7).

See further 14:20. God refuses to respond to the prayer of him who neglects or mistreats the poor, but blesses him who helps the needy.

> "He who closes his ear to the cry of the poor
> will himself cry out and not be heard" (21:13).

> "He who has a bountiful eye will be blessed,
> for he shares his bread with the poor"
> (22:9; see also 28:27).

The Diligent and the Sluggard

The book of Proverbs emphasizes the necessity and importance of hard work in the life of a righteous man, and condemns laziness as a fundamental characteristic of wicked men. He who works regularly and diligently will naturally receive the fruits of his labor.

> "Know well the condition of your flocks,
> and give attention to your herds;
> for riches do not last for ever;
> and does a crown endure to all generations?
> When the grass is gone, and the new growth appears,
> and the herbage of the mountains is gathered,
> the lambs will provide your clothing,
> and the goats the price of a field;
> there will be enough goats' milk for your food,
> for the food of your household
> and maintenance for your maidens" (27:23-27).

See 27:18; I Corinthians 9:6-14; I Timothy 5:17-18.

100

One who is lazy may want something very badly, but he does not get it because he is too lazy to work for it.

"The soul of the sluggard craves, and gets nothing,
while the soul of the diligent is richly supplied"
(13:4).

"The desire of the sluggard kills him, for his hands refuse to labor."

See further 21:25. It is one thing to talk about how hard one works or wants to work, and an entirely different thing to actually work hard.

"In all toil there is profit,
but mere talk tends only to want" (14:23).

It is just as sinful to be slothful and fail to provide for the needs of one's own family as it would be to destroy that family.

"He who is slack in his work
is a brother to him who destroys"
(18:9; see I Timothy 5:8).

"If anyone does not provide for his relatives, and especially for his own family, he has disowned the faith and is worse than an un- believer. (infidel)"

Diligence involves taking advantage of one's opportunities when they arise. "He who hesitates is lost."

"The sluggard does not plow in the autumn;
he will seek at harvest and have nothing"
(20:4).

"Look carefully then how you walk, not as unwise men but as wise, making the most of the time, because the days are evil."

See Ephesians 5:15-16; Colossians 4:5-6; Hebrews 5:12-14. The reason the sluggard does not make progress or accomplish anything substantial is that he is afraid to try anything, knowing subconsciously down deep in his heart that he does not really plan to pursue it to its completion.

"The sluggard says, 'There is a lion outside! I shall be slain in the streets!'"

"The sluggard says, 'There is a lion in the road!
There is a lion in the streets!'" (26:13).

Also see 22:13. Accordingly, the slothful person is a laughingstock to those about him, yet he cannot see how foolish he looks.

"As a door turns on its hinges,
so does a sluggard on his bed.
The sluggard buries his hand in the dish;
it wears him out to bring it back to his mouth.

The sluggard is wiser in his own eyes
than seven men who can answer discreetly"
(26:14-16).

See further 19:24.

"The sluggard buries his hand in the dish,
and will not even bring it back to his mouth."

Review Questions

1. List the seven contrasts between the wise and the fool- *p 93-95*
ish mentioned in this lesson. Discuss each of these at
length. From your own reading of the book of Proverbs, add other contrasts between the wise and the
foolish not mentioned in this chapter. Let each
member of the class contribute what he has found.

2. Using James 1:19-20 as your guideline, discuss the
importance of being slow to speak and slow to anger.
Are there certain groups in society which are more
guilty of the sins of responding immediately in speech
and with anger? Discuss.   *(some) politicians!*

3. In light of Proverbs 10:12; 20:3, discuss the problem
of strife and division among God's people. What is the
real source of strife and division? What can be done
about this?

4. Name four ways one can become wealthy. Proverbs
19:14; 21:6; 10:4; 3:9-10. Discuss each of these. Enumerate five ways one can become poor. Proverbs
13:23, 21, 18; 28:19; 23:20-21. Discuss each of these.
Now contrast those things which lead to riches with
those which lead to poverty.

5. Does the Bible condemn wealth in itself? When does
wealth become wrong? Proverbs 11:28. Name four
things which are much more valuable than great
riches. Proverbs 20:15; 22:1; 16:8; 3:13-15. Discuss this
concept.

6. Discuss the responsibility of the rich toward the poor.
Proverbs 14:31; 19:4; 21:13; 22:9.

7. What does each of the following passages teach about
laziness? Proverbs 14:23; 18:9; 20:4; 26:13-16. Discuss
the biblical teaching on work and laziness.

FAMILY, FRIENDS, AND COMMUNITY

"Righteousness exalts a nation,
but sin is a reproach to any people" (Proverbs 14:34).

Like all nations, Israel was guilty of various kinds of sin and corruption in the family, between friends, and in government. But this was not pleasing to God. Through inspired speakers and writers he called for a stable, solid, godly family life as the backbone of a wholesome and productive community, city, and nation. A major emphasis in the book of Proverbs is on the responsibilities of the various members of the family, fidelity in friendship, and the duties of rulers to citizens and of citizens to rulers. These concerns are the subject of the present lesson. Here there is also a brief treatment of the Song of Solomon because of its teaching concerning the marriage relationship.

The Family

There is a very strong emphasis on the necessity of fidelity in marriage both in Proverbs and in the Song of Solomon. Song of Solomon has been interpreted in a number of ways. (1) Some think the husband is God and the wife Israel. (2) Others believe the husband is Christ and the wife his church. (3) A few scholars have found a romantic triangle in the book. Solomon has taken a young woman as a wife, but she is actually in love with a poor shepherd. Song of Solomon tells of some of their secret romantic meetings. (4) It has been suggested that this book describes premarital or extramarital sex. (5) However, the most natural interpretation is that it describes the strong sexual attractions and activities of a newly married couple. The man calls the woman "my sister, my bride" (Song of Solomon 4:9, 10, 12; 5:1).

God created man male and female in order that each might have a strong sexual attraction for the other (Genesis 2:18-25). Sexual pleasure and enjoyment is a good thing within the marriage relationship, and Song of Solomon extols this. Both the man and the woman are wholly satisfied with the physical beauty of the other, and do not hesitate to express that satisfaction and to engage in love-making. The woman describes her husband in this way.

> "My beloved is all radiant and ruddy, *describes from head, down*
> distinguished among ten thousand.
> His head is the finest gold;
> his locks are wavy,
> black as a raven.
> His eyes are like doves
> beside springs of water,
> bathed in milk,
> fitly set.
> His cheeks are like beds of spices,
> yielding fragrance.
> His lips are lilies,
> distilling liquid myrrh.
> His arms are rounded gold,
> set with jewels.
> His body is ivory work,
> encrusted with sapphires.
> His legs are alabaster columns,
> set upon bases of gold.
> His appearance is like Lebanon,
> choice as the cedars.
> His speech is most sweet,
> and he is altogether desirable.
> This is my beloved and this is my friend,
> O daughters of Jerusalem" (Song of Solomon 5:10-16).

Reciprocally, the man describes his wife with these words.

describes from feet, up

"How graceful are your feet in sandals,
O queenly maiden!
Your rounded thighs are like jewels,
the work of a master hand.
Your navel is a rounded bowl
that never lacks mixed wine.
Your belly is a heap of wheat,
encircled with lilies.
Your two breasts are like two fawns,
twins of a gazelle.
Your neck is like an ivory tower.
Your eyes are pools in Heshbon,
by the gate of Bath-rabbim.
Your nose is like a tower of Lebanon,
overlooking Damascus.
Your head crowns you like Carmel,
and your flowing locks are like purple;
a king is held captive in the tresses" (7:1-5).

It is this sort of mutual attraction and appreciation
which Paul extols in passages like I Corinthians 7:3-5. *Important*
Such feelings and experiences are one of the strongest
deterrents to infidelity in marriage and to extramarital
affairs.

The book of Proverbs contains numerous admonitions
to the young man to be satisfied with his wife's love,
and to avoid the temptations of an adulteress or a prostitute. For example, the wise man instructs:

"Drink water from your own cistern,
flowing water from your own well.
Should your springs be scattered abroad,
streams of water in the streets?
Let them be for yourself alone,
and not for strangers with you.
Let your fountain be blessed,
and rejoice in the wife of your youth,
a lovely hind, a graceful doe.
Let her affection fill you at all times with delight,
be infatuated always with her love.

Why should you be infatuated,
my son, with a loose woman
and embrace the bosom of an adventuress?"
(Proverbs 5:15-20).

In another place he gives this vivid description.
"For at the window of my house
I have looked out through my lattice,
and I have seen among the simple,
I have perceived among the youths,
a young man without sense,
passing along the street near her corner,
taking the road to her house
in the twilight, in the evening,
at the time of night and darkness.
And lo, a woman meets him,
dressed as a harlot, wily of heart.
She is loud and wayward,
her feet do not stay at home;
now in the street, now in the market,
and at every corner she lies in wait.
She seizes him and kisses him,
and with impudent face she says to him:
'I had to offer sacrifices,
and today I have paid my vows:
so now I have come out to meet you,
to seek you eagerly, and I have found you.
I have decked my couch with coverings,
colored spreads of Egyptian linen;
I have perfumed my bed with myrrh,
aloes, and cinnamon.
Come, let us take our fill of love till morning;
let us delight ourselves with love.
For my husband is not at home;
he has gone on a long journey;
he took a bag of money with him;
at full moon he will come home.'
With much seductive speech she persuades him;
with her smooth talk she compels him.
All at once he follows her,

as   an   ox   goes   to   the   slaughter,
or   as   a   stag   is   caught   fast
till   an   arrow   pierces   its   entrails;
as   a   bird   rushes   into   a   snare;
he   does   not   know   that   it   will   cost   him   his   life"
(7:6-23).

See   also   6:20-35.

THE FAMILY
(1,2,#3)

1. *Husband and Wife.* The husband is to be faithful to his wife, constantly manifest his love for her, and provide for all of her needs (see the passages above, and the passages on diligence and work in Lesson X). A godly wife is no accident, but is a gift of the Lord to the husband.

"House   and   wealth   are   inherited   from   fathers,
but   a   prudent   wife   is   from   the   Lord"
(19:14;   see   also   18:22).

Thus it is logical and important for a young man to pray fervently and constantly to the Lord as he looks for a wife, and to study God's word carefully as he seeks the qualities which a Christian wife should possess; and for a young woman to do likewise as she looks for a husband. Of course, this is not to imply God chooses a particular woman for a particular man. Several passages in the book of Proverbs decry the miserable situation of a man having to live with a quarrelsome and contentious wife.

"A   foolish   son   is   ruin   to   his   father,
and   a   wife's   quarreling   is   a   continual   *"15 a continual dropping on a rainy day and a contentious*
dripping   of   rain"   (19:13).   *woman are alike; to restrain her is to restrain the*
wind or to grasp oil in his right hand."
See   further   21:9, 19;   25:24;   27:15-16.   The   wife   who desires   to   be   a   genuine   helper   to   her   husband   should take   careful   note   of   these   admonitions.

In contrast to many ancient Near Eastern societies, true Israelites did not regard a woman as an impersonal possession whose father or husband could treat her any way he desired, and who catered to every whim and fancy of the men in her family. Rather, she was highly honored as one created in the image of God equally as much as a man. And in the family she had her unique and honorable functions to perform just as did her husband. The famous acrostic poem on the "good wife" in Proverbs 31:10-31 emphasizes this concept. It describes the ideal wife as (1) trustworthy (vs. 11); (2) always helpful to her mate (vs. 12); (3) a willing worker (vs. 13); (4) one who is careful in purchasing goods for her household (vs. 14); (5) one who rises early to provide the daily needs for her household (vss. 15, 21-22, 27); (6) a good business woman (vss. 16, 24); (7) one who strives to remain healthy (vss. 18-19, 31); (9) generous and hospitable to the poor and needy (vs. 20); (10) one who encourages and supports her husband in his work (vs. 23); (11) a wise counselor and teacher (vs. 26); (12) kind (vs. 26); (13) one who is respected and appreciated by her husband and children (vss. 28-29); and (14) one who fears the Lord (vs. 30). See also 11:16; 12:4.

2. *Parent and Child.* God gave children parents for a reason. The fundamental responsibility of the parent is to raise his child in a godly environment for service to God and his fellowmen.

"Train up a child in the way he should go,
and when he is old he will not depart from it" (22:6).

This involves both teaching the child and being an example for him.

"A righteous man who walks in his integrity—
blessed are his sons after him!" (20:7).

A godly man leaves an inheritance to his descendants, since it is the responsibility of parents to provide for the future of their children and not children for their parents.

"A good man leaves an inheritance to his children's children,
but the sinner's wealth is laid up for the righteous" (13:22).

See also II Corinthians 12:14. The book of Proverbs

"Here for th' third time I am ready to come to you. And I will not be a burden, for I seek not what is yours but you; for children ought not to lay up for their parents, but parents for their children."

stresses the importance of correcting children when they do what they should not, and this correction includes spanking (not to be confused with or identified with "child beating").

> "He who spares the rod hates his son,
> but he who loves him is diligent to discipline him" (13:24).

> "Folly is bound up in the heart of a child,
> but the rod of discipline drives it far from him" (22:15).

> "Do not withhold discipline from a child;
> if you beat him with a rod, he will not die.
> if you beat him with the rod
> you will save his life from Sheol" (23:13-14).

"Discipline your son while there is hope; do not set your heart on his destruction."

See further 19:18; 29:15, 17. *The rod and reproof give wisdom, but a child left to himself brings shame to his mother."*

"Discipline your son, and he will give you rest; he will give delight to your heart."

Children of righteous parents must strive to reflect in their own lives the environment and training which they have received in the home in which they were raised. Certainly this does not mean they are to agree with their parents on everything, or pursue the occupation most desired by their parents, or live where their parents would prefer, and the like. Rather, they are to serve God with their whole hearts and love their neighbors as themselves, thus indicating that the godly influence of their parents was effective.

> "The father of the righteous will greatly rejoice;
> he who begets a wise son will be glad in him.
> Let your father and mother be glad,
> let her who bore you rejoice" (23:24-25).

As was pointed out in Lesson II, "a wise son" is one who fears God and departs from evil. On this, see further 10:1; 15:20; 17:21, 25, 27:11. A wise son will listen to his parents' advice, knowing it comes from those who love him most dearly, have invested the most time and money in his life, and are concerned with what is best for him.

A wise son makes a glad father, but a foolish man is a sorrow to his mother.

> "Hearken to your father who begot you,
> and do not despise your mother when she is old" (23:22).

30:17 The eye that mocks a father and scorns to obey a mother will be picked out by the ravens of the valley and eaten by the vultures."

20:20 If one curses his father or his mother, his lamp will be put out in utter darkness."

"A wise son hears his father's instruction, but a scoffer does not listen to rebuke."

See also 13:1. In light of this very high esteem in which a child is to hold his parents, the book of Proverbs specifically condemns certain sins which one might commit against his parents: (a) gluttony and running with gluttons (28:7); (b) treating one's parents violently or harshly (19:26); (c) robbing one's parents (28:24); (d) mocking and scorning to obey one's parents (30:17); and (e) cursing one's parents (20:20). *"He who robs his father or his mother and says, 'That is no transgression,' is the companion of a man who destroys."*

How about grandparents? & rob not just of physical but of mental too. Not really robbery but by words ... is it coercement? "I won't love you if you don't give me what I want!"

3. *Master and Servant.* Both among the Israelites in Old Testament times and among Christians in the first century A.D. (see for example, I Corinthians 7:20-24; Ephesians 6:5-9; Colossians 3:22-4:1), it was quite common to have servants or slaves as members of the household. However, genuine Israelites and Christians did not think of or treat their servants as things or impersonal possessions, but as dignified human beings made in the image of God. This is reflected in statements concerning the roles of masters and slaves in the book of Proverbs. As long as one is a slave (usually seven years—see Exodus 21:2-6), he should be content with his duties in this position and not try to assume a role for which he is not suited.

"It is not fitting for a fool to live in luxury,
much less for a slave to rule over princes" (19:10).

Sometimes it is necessary to use more severe measures than mere words to get a servant to do his work.

"By mere words a servant is not disciplined,
for though he understands, he will not give heed"
(29:19).

See also 29:21. One must not slander a servant to his master. In fact, all slander is wrong (see Lesson XII).

"Do not slander a servant to his master,
lest he curse you, and you be held guilty"
(30:17).

A slave who is conscientious and loyal, and works hard for his master will be greatly blessed.

111

"A slave who deals wisely will rule over a son,
who acts shamefully,
and will share the inheritance as one of the
brothers" (17:2).

*There are friends who pretend to be friends, but there is a friend
who sticks closer than a brother."*

Friendship

The book of Proverbs contains some interesting instructions concerning those who pretend to be friends but are not. (1) If one learns someone is wealthy, he will become his friend in the hope of gaining some benefit for himself (19:4, 6-7). (2) One should be cautious about making friends quickly, because relatively few friends will be loyal in all circumstances (18:24). (3) It is dangerous to become friends with someone who is easily angered, because one will become like he is (22:24-25).

quoted on p. 100 (at top)

24 "Make no friendship with a man given to anger, nor go with a wrathful man,
25 lest you learn his ways and entangle yourself in a snare."

There are also some very important thoughts regarding true friendship in this Old Testament book. (1) A genuine friend will be faithful in adversity as well as in prosperity.

"A friend loves at all times,
and a brother is born for adversity"
(17:17; see also 18:24).

(2) A true friend is often more faithful in times of calamity than a member of one's own family. *TRUE!*

"Your friend, and your father's friend,
do not forsake;
and do not go to your brother's house
in the day of your calamity.
Better is a neighbor who is near
than a brother who is far away" (27:10).

(3) A real friend is more concerned with what is best for his friend than with preserving the friendship. Therefore, if it is necessary, he will rebuke his friend for planning to do or for doing the wrong thing.

"Better is open rebuke
than hidden love.

Faithful are the wounds of a friend;
profuse are the kisses of an enemy" (27:5-6).

(4) Thus a true friend improves his friend's character.
"Iron sharpens iron,
and one man sharpens another" (27:17).

Ruler and Citizen

The very nature of human life on earth demands some
sort of organized government that all may survive and
be reasonably blessed. Therefore, the book of Proverbs
has a great deal to say about the responsibilities of
rulers to those under them. First, the ruler must realize
he himself is subject to God and his will, and that he is
God's representative among his people.

"The king's heart is a stream of water in the
hand of the Lord;
he (that is, God) turns it wherever he will"
(21:1).

Second, a major concern of the ruler with regard to
internal affairs is to make sure everyone is treated
justly.

"When the righteous are in authority, the people
rejoice;
but when the wicked rule, the people groan" (29:2).

"By justice a king gives stability to the land,
but one who exacts gifts ruins it" (29:4).

See further 14:34-35; 16:10, 12; 17:7; 20:8, 28; 25:2-5;
29:12, 14. So in court trials, witnesses must not be
vengeful (24:28-29) or bear false witness for any reason
(12:17; 14:25; 19:5; 21:28; 25:18), and judges must not
accept bribes (15:27; 17:23; 18:5; 28:21) or deliberately
render wrong verdicts (17:26; 24:24-26). Third, a good
king will punish the wicked in harmony with the serious-
ness of his crime in order to rehabilitate him if at all

"A false witness will
not go unpunished,
and he who utters lies
will not escape."

"A man who bears false witness against his neighbor
is like a war club, or a sword, or a sharp arrow."

"A false witness will perish,
but the word of a man who hears will endure."

113

possible and to protect the other members of the community.

> "A wise king winnows the wicked,
> and drives the wheel over them" (20:26).

Fourth, the ruler must associate with the people constantly in order that he might stay in touch with their needs and problems.

> "A ruler who lacks understanding is a cruel oppressor;
> but he who hates unjust gain will prolong his days" (28:16).

Also see 28:2, 15; 29:14; 31:8-9. Fifth and finally, a good ruler will refrain from strong drink in order that he may be alert to help his people at any time when problems arise.

> "It is not for kings, O Lemuel,
> it is not for kings to drink wine,
> or for rulers to desire strong drink;
> lest they drink and forget what has been decreed,
> and pervert the rights of all the afflicted" (31:4-5).

Likewise, godly citizens will accept their role of responsibility to their rulers and to each other. (a) Citizens must hold God and the king in the highest respect.

> "My son, fear the Lord and the king,
> and do not disobey either of them" (24:21).

See also Romans 13:1-7; I Peter 2:13-17. (b) The people should support righteous rulers in every way (14:28). (c) Citizens must assume the responsibility for living righteous lives themselves that the community or nation might be strong (11:10-11; 14:34). (d) One must be humble and respectful before rulers.

> "With patience a ruler may be persuaded,
> and a soft tongue will break a bone"
> (25:15; see also 25:6-7).

"Righteousness exalts a nation, but sin is a reproach to any people."

114

Review Questions

1. Give five interpretations of a Song of Solomon. Discuss the pros and cons of each position. Which do you think is correct? See Song of Solomon 4:9, 10, 12, 5:1.

2. Discuss the biblical teaching on what should be one's attitude toward sexual activity within and outside of marriage. Song of Solomon 5:10-16; 7:1-5; I Corinthians 7:3-5; Proverbs 5:15-20; 6:20-35; 7:6-23.

3. List the characteristics of a good wife given in Proverbs 31:10-31. Discuss each of these.

4. What is the major responsibility of a parent toward his child? Proverbs 22:6. Discuss the role of disciplining the child in light of this responsibility. See Proverbs 13:24; 23:13-14.

5. Enumerate five specific sins a child may commit against his parents which are condemned in the book of Proverbs. Proverbs 28:7; 19:26; 28:24; 30:17; 20:20. Discuss each of these.

6. Discuss four characteristics of a true friend. Proverbs 17:17; 27:20, 5-6, 17. Contrast these with characteristics of those who pretend to be friends but are not. Proverbs 19:4, 6-7; 18:24; 22:24-25.

7. List and discuss five characteristics of a good ruler. Proverbs 21:1; 29:2; 20:26; 28:16; 31:4-5.

8. Name four qualities godly citizens of a community or a nation should possess. Proverbs 24:21; 14:28; 11:10-11; 25:15.

Lesson XII

RESPONSIBILITIES TO GOD, SELF, AND OTHERS

"Let not your heart envy sinners,
but continue in the fear of the Lord all the day"
(Proverbs 23:17)

The book of Proverbs is rich in teaching concerning the individual's responsibilities to God, to himself, and to his fellowmen. There is so much material in this biblical book on these areas, in fact, that they cannot be treated exhaustively in a single lesson. Therefore, the present lesson treats only a few of the concepts presented in Proverbs.

Man's Responsibilities to God

In essence, the proper response of man to God's powerful, loving works in his behalf is to "fear" him, that is, to hold him in the highest respect (1:7; 8:13; 9:10; 15:33; 16:6; 28:14 — see Lesson II). From this basic principle come certain specific responsibilities. (1) One must trust God with his whole heart.

"Trust in the Lord with all your heart,
and do not rely on your own insight.
In all your ways acknowledge him,
and he will make straight your paths" (3:5-6).

Also see 16:20; 28:25-26; 29:25. (2) The godly person is to be humble before God (3:7-8; 22:4; 28:11). (3) He must respect and obey God's commandments.

"He who despises the word brings destruction on himself, *"The reward for humility and fear of the LORD is riches and honor and life."*

116

but he who respects the commandment will be
rewarded" (13:13).

See further 28:4, 7, 9; 29:18. (4) The righteous is to
accept divine discipline as a manifestation of God's love
to him to help him grow spiritually (3:11-12). (5) He who
genuinely fears the Lord will strive to live a righteous
life (14:2). (6) Gratitude for God's gifts leads the godly
individual to offer a portion of his possessions to God.

"Honor the Lord with you substance
and with the first fruits of all your produce;
then your barns will be filled with plenty,
and your vats will be bursting with wine" (3:9-10).

But animal or vegetable sacrifices or any other gift one
brings to God must come from one whose heart and
daily life are in harmony with his profession (15:8;
21:27). (7) Since the godly man is in constant communion
with God and totally dependent on him, it is very important for him to pray at all times (15:8, 29; 28:9).

The Individual's Responsibilities to Himself

The adult human being is free to make his own
decisions and to live his own life. But this carries with it
the responsibilities one must accept for his own actions,
and the willingness to accept the fruits which God has
ordained for various ways of life. God is greatly concerned about each individual, and he desires that each
person have a high regard for his own spiritual well-
being. Consequently the Bible, and certainly the book of
Proverbs, urges each person to develop certain attitudes
and patterns of behavior which will build him up rather
than tear him down and destroy him. For sake of
convenience, these may be grouped under three
categories.

1. *Right Motives.* Jesus emphasized that it is possible to
do right things externally but to have wrong motives in
the heart for doing them (see for example, Matthew 5:21-
48). The book of Proverbs teaches the same truth.

"Keep your heart with all vigilance;
for from it flow the springs of life" (4:23).

"He who loves purity of heart,
and whose speech is gracious,
will have the king as his friend" (22:11).

"The righteousness of the upright delivers them,
but the treacherous are taken captive by their lust"
(11:6).

*The righteousness of the blameless keeps his way straight,
but the wicked falls by his own wickedness."*

See further 11:5, 23, 27; 13:6; 21:8, 10.

*"The desire of the righteous ends only in good;
the expectation of the wicked in wrath."*   *"The way of the guilty is crooked,
but the conduct of the pure is right."*

2. *Attitude toward temptation.* It is easy for a person
to underestimate the power of temptation. Many have
boasted of their ability to resist and overcome any and
all temptations, only to find themselves hopelessly
entangled in sin. In light of this, the book of Proverbs
contains many admonitions to take temptation very
seriously, to be constantly aware of its attempts to over-
throw the righteous, and to realize how dangerous it is
to one's spiritual well-being. (1) It is foolish to play with
or court temptation. The wise thing is to flee from it.

"A wise man is cautious and turns away from evil,
but a fool throws off restraint and is careless" (14:16).

"Be not envious of evil men,
nor desire to be with them;
for their minds devise violence,
and their lips talk of mischief" (24:1-2)

"A prudent man sees danger and hides himself;
but the simple go on, and suffer for it" (27:12).

See also 4:14-17, 25-27; 21:29. (2) Resist temptation when
it first appears, because it will be too late to overcome it
if it is allowed to grow and grip one's heart.

"The beginning of strife is like letting out water;
so quit before the quarrel breaks out" (17:14).

(3) By yielding to temptation one corrupts the purity of
his whole-hearted commitment to God.

"Like a muddied spring or a polluted fountain

is a righteous man who gives way before the wicked"
(25:26).

3. *Self-Control.* A basic characteristic of human nature
is the ability to see and to criticize the faults in others,
but the inability to see and overcome one's own sins. The
book of Proverbs discusses a number of things in one's
own life over which it is necessary to exercise self-
control. (a) It is necessary to control one's eating habits.
Gluttony is sin.

"Be not among winebibbers,
or among gluttonous eaters of meat;
for the drunkard and the glutton will come to poverty,
and drowsiness will clothe a man with rags"

If you have found honey, eat only enough for you,
lest you be sated with it and vomit it."

(23:20-21).

See further 25:16; Deuteronomy 21:18-21. (b) One must
restrain himself from drinking intoxicating beverages.
Drunkenness is sin.

"Who has woe? Who has sorrow?
Who has strife? Who has complaining?
Who has wounds without cause?
Who has redness of eyes?
Those who tarry long over wine,
those who go to try mixed wine.
Do not look at wine when it is red,
when it sparkles in the cup
and goes down smoothly.
At the last it bites like a serpent,
and stings like an adder.
Your eyes will see strange things,
and your mind utter perverse things.
You will be like one who lies down in the midst of
the sea, like one who lies on the top of a mast.
'They struck me,' you will say, 'but I was not hurt;
they beat me, but I did not feel it.
When shall I awake? *"Wine is a mocker, strong drink a brawler;*
and whoever is led astray by it is not wise."
I will seek another drink.'" (23:29-35; see also 20:1).

(c) A godly man must be moderate in his sleeping
habits. Too much sleep bespeaks laziness, and prevents

119

one from using his energies in service to God and his fellowmen to their fullest capacity.

"Love not sleep, lest you come to poverty;
open your eyes, and you will have plenty of
bread" (20:13).

Also see 6:6-11; 24:30-34; and Lesson X on Laziness. (d) It is important to control one's desire to engage in sexual pleasure not intended by the Creator, that is, any sexual activity outside wholesome heterosexual marriage.

"He who loves wisdom makes his father glad,
but one who keeps company with harlots
squanders his substance" (29:3).

See also 6:20-35; 7:6-23; 21:17; 23:26-28; 31:3; and Lesson XI on the Family. (e) The righteous person will endeavor to control his tongue (see below on A Person's Responsibilities to Others). He will refrain from talking too much, and will be very careful about what he says.

"When words are many, transgression is not lacking,
but he who restrains his lips is prudent" (10:19).

"He who keeps his mouth and his tongue
keeps himself out of trouble" (21:23).

See in addition 13:3; 18:21. (f) A godly man must learn to control his anger.

"He who is slow to anger is better than the mighty,
and he who rules his spirit than he who takes a city"
(16:32).

"A man without self-control
is like a city
broken into and left without walls" (25:28).

"A fool gives full vent to his anger,
but a wise man quietly holds it back" (29:11).

See further 14:17; 17:27-28; 19:11. (g) He who would serve God must develop the self-discipline to hear all the evidence and to weigh it carefully before he reaches a decision. Quick, on-the-spot decisions are often wrong.

"If one gives answer before he hears,
it is his folly and shame" (18:13)

(h) Rash religious promises made when one is caught up in the emotion of some sort of enthusiastic fervor do not characterize the righteous person.

"It is a snare for a man to say rashly, 'It is holy,' and to reflect only after making his vows" (20:25).

For more explicit details on this point, see Numbers 30:2-16; Deuteronomy 23:21-23.

A Person's Responsibility to Others

The responsibilities which a godly person has toward others may be divided into three broad categories.

1. *Attitudes.* It is wrong to have a negative, suspicious attitude toward others. Surely all have sinned and fall short of the glory of God, but this should provide all the more reason to be understanding of others. After all, they are faced with the same problems of thinking positively toward us. (a) The book of Proverbs teaches that one must love his neighbor and not hate him.

"Hatred stirs up strife,
but love covers all offenses" (10:12).

"He who despises his neighbor is a sinner,
but happy is he who is kind to the poor" (14:21).

See also 15:17. (b) The righteous person will ponder in his heart prayerfully and carefully how he is to respond to what others say and do. In other words, he will be genuinely concerned not to hurt his fellowman.

"The mind of the righteous ponders how to answer,
but the mouth of the wicked pours out evil things" (15:28).

(c) A godly individual has a forgiving heart toward one who has wronged him, and ever stands ready to forgive and forget.

"He who forgives an offense seeks love,
but he who repeats a matter alienates a friend" (17:9).

121

(d) The man of God does not envy the notoriety or possessions of others, but is content with his own blessings from God.

"Fret not yourself because of evildoers,
and be not envious of the wicked;
for the evil man has no future;
the lamp of the wicked will be put out" (24:19-20).

See also 21:26; 23:17-18; 24:1-2; 27:4

[handwritten: "Wrath is cruel, anger is overwhelming; but who can stand before jealousy?"]

[handwritten left margin: "All day long the wicked covets, but the righteous gives and does not hold back."]

2. Speech. God is very concerned about man's use of his tongue. God created the tongue to praise Him and to build up one's fellows.

"Anxiety in a man's heart weighs him down,
but a good word makes him glad" (12:25).

"A word fitly spoken
is like apples of gold in a setting of silver" (25:11).

[handwritten: "a gentle tongue is a tree of life, but perverseness in it breaks the spirit."]

See further 10:11; 12:18; 15:4; 16:24. But man often uses the tongue in ways which are destructive to himself and particularly to others. Several sins of the tongue are condemned in the book of Proverbs.

[handwritten: "Pleasant words are like a honeycomb, sweetness to the soul and health to the body."]

(a) Lying and deceit.

"Truthful lips endure for ever,
but a lying tongue is but for a moment" (12:19).

See also 6:16-19; 10:18; 12:17, 20, 22; 14:5; 17:4, 7; 19:5, 9; 21:28; 25:18; 26:28.

[handwritten: "He who conceals hatred has lying lips, and he who utters slander is a fool."]

(b) Boasting.

[handwritten: "a lying tongue hates its victims, and a flattering mouth works ruin."]

"Let another praise you, and not your own mouth;
a stranger, and not your own lips"
(27:2; see 25:14; 27:1).

(c) Belittling one's neighbor.

"He who belittles his neighbor lacks sense,
but a man of understanding remains silent" (11:12).

(d) Anger or harshness.

"A soft answer turns away wrath,
but a harsh word stirs up anger" (15:1).

See also 25:23; 29:11.

(e) Rashness.

"There is one whose rash words are like sword thrusts, but the tongue of the wise brings healing" (12:18).

Further see 29:20.

(f) Flattery, that is, praising someone without really believing he is worthy of such praise for the purpose of getting or staying in his favor and of getting praise or favors from him in return.

"A lying tongue hates its victims,
and a flattering mouth works ruin" (26:28).

"He who rebukes a man will afterward find more favor than he who flatters with his tongue" (28:23).

See in addition 19:6; 29:5.

(g) Gossip. The book of Proverbs condemns both telling and listening to gossip.

"He who goes about as a talebearer reveals secrets, but he who is trustworthy in spirit keeps a thing hidden" (11:13).

"A perverse man spreads strife,
and a whisperer separates close friends" (16:28).

"Argue your case with your neighbor himself,
and do not disclose another's secret;
lest he who hears you bring shame upon you,
and your ill repute have no end" (25:9-10).

"He who goes about gossiping reveals secrets;
therefore do not associate with one who speaks foolishly" (20:19).

Also see 18:8; 26:20-22.

(h) Slander. Slander is a vicious form of gossip, in which one uses either truth or error for the purpose of trying to harm his fellowman.

"He who conceals hatred has lying lips,
and he who utters slander is a fool" (10:18).

In addition to the passages above on Gossip, see Romans 1:28-32; Ephesians 4:31-32; Colossians 3:5-8. Lev. 19:16

3. *Actions.* A righteous person will behave toward his fellowman in a godlike manner. According to the book of Proverbs, this involves some very significant specific actions. (a) He must use discretion as to how often he goes to see his neighbor.

"Let your foot be seldom in your neighbor's house,
Lest he become weary of you and hate you" (25:17).

(b) The godly person is to refrain from meddling in other people's business.

"He who meddles in a quarrel not his own
is like one who takes a passing dog by the ears"
(26:17)

(c) He will help those who are in need.

"Do not withhold good from those to whom it is due,
when it is your power to do it.
Do not say to your neighbor, 'Go, and come again,
tomorrow I will give it' — when you have it with you"
(3:27-28).

"He who is kind to the poor lends to the Lord,
and he will repay him for his deed" (19:17).

Also see 11:24-26; 14:21, 31; 17:5; 21:26. (d) The righteous returns good for evil, which tends to bring peace between himself and the one who has wronged him.

"If your enemy is hungry, give him bread to eat;
and if he is thirsty, give him water to drink;
for you will heap coals of fire on his head,
and the Lord will reward you" (25:21-22; see Romans
12:17-21).

"Do not rejoice when your enemy falls,
and let not your heart be glad when he stumbles;
lest the Lord see it, and be displeased,
and turn away his anger from him" (24:17-18).

"Do not say, 'I will do to him as he has done to me;
I will pay the man back for what he has done.'"
(24:29).

See in addition 17:13; 20:22; Matthew 5:38-48; I Peter 3:9.

Review   Questions

1. Enumerate seven proper responses man should make to God mighty deeds, love, and mercy toward him as stated in the book of Proverbs. Proverbs 3:5-6, 7-8; 13:13; 3:11-12; 14:2; 3:9-10; 15:8. Discuss each of these.

2. Why are right motives important in every aspect of the life of a godly person? Proverbs 4:23. Discuss at length.

3. In teaching the righteous how to deal with temptation, what three important lessons does the book of Proverbs teach? Proverbs 4:14-17; 17:14; 25:26. Discuss each of these.

4. List eight things the book of Proverbs says one must control in his life. Proverbs 23:20-21, 29-35; 20:13; 29:3; 10:19; 29:11; 18:13; 20:25. Choose the three of these with which you have the greatest problem, share this with the class, and discuss how you might actually begin gaining control over these problems in your own personal   life.

5. What four basic attitudes must one have toward others according to the book of Proverbs? Proverbs 10:12; 15:28; 17:9; 24:19-20. With what two of these do you have the greatest difficulty? Discuss with the other members of the class how you might change your attitudes   toward   others.

6. Enumerate eight sins of the tongue which are condemned in the book of Proverbs. Proverbs 12:19; 27:1-2; 11:12; 15:1; 12:18; 28:23; 25:9-10; 10:18. Which two of these sins do you think are most prevalent in the world today? Which two do you think are most prevalent in the church? Discuss at lengh. What can be done about this?

7. The book of Proverbs discusses at least four ways a godly person is supposed to behave toward his fellowman. Name them. Proverbs 25:17; 26:17; 3:27-28; 25:21-22. Discuss each of these, and share with the class your failures and successes in this area.

Stoic: a member of a Greek school of philosophy founded by Zeno about 308 B.C., holding that men should be free from passion and should calmly accept all occurrences as the unavoidable result of divine will.

Lesson XIII

"ALL IS VANITY" (ECCLESIASTES)

"All is vanity and a striving after wind"
(Ecclesiastes 2:17).

The book of Ecclesiastes is very difficult to understand. Scholars interpret this work in a wide variety of ways. (1) Some think its author is a pessimist. Repeatedly he cries out, "Vanity of vanities! All is vanity" (1:2, 14; 2:17, 23, 26; and so forth). But his purpose here seems to be to emphasize that all things of this world are vain so that man will not trust in them. (2) It has been suggested that the writer was a Stoic, because of the emphasis on the vanity of man's life and work, contempt for the world, and the view that all weaknesses are a form of insanity. However, the author's purpose in speaking of these matters apparently is to show that they fail to supply or provide that for which man yearns and seeks. (3) Others believe the author was an Epicurean, because he repeatedly gives the advice to "eat, drink, and be merry" (2:24-25 and several other passages — see below under "Victorious Living"). Yet he does not have in mind sensuous pleasure, but wholesome enjoyment of the gifts God has placed on earth for man to enjoy. (4) Some suppose the writer was a skeptic, as he emphasizes man's inability to comprehend God's ways, the futility of things on earth to satisfy man's desires, and the brevity of life on earth. But a proper realization of these truths will ultimately lead an individual to trust in God and in him alone. (5) The viewpoint which appears to be most in keeping with the overall thrust of the book and its contents is that nothing in this world satisfies the deep needs and longings of man, no matter how good and wholesome they are in themselves, and therefore man must look beyond this world to God to find ultimate fulfillment and satisfaction in life (see 12:13-14).

Analyzing the Book of Ecclesiastes

Various experts view the structure and flow of thought in the book of Ecclesiastes in a number of ways. (1) Some think the original author was a thoroughgoing pessimist, who believed that everything in life is vain. Accordingly, the passages which are optimistic are understood as glosses and assigned to a later editor who was displeased with the earlier pessimistic viewpoint. (2) Others find a dialogue in the book between a pessimist and an optimist, and thus assign the different passages to one speaker or the other. (3) Still others compare Ecclesiastes with Proverbs, and view it basically as an incoherent collection of brief wisdom sayings, each of which is to be studied in isolation and not as a basic contributing factor to a well worked out theme in the book. (4) It seems most likely that the book of Ecclesiastes is a coherent unity, whose author looks at various aspects of life, now from an earthly perspective, now from God's perspective. His purpose is to help man see the great limitations of human strength and understanding in the hope that he will turn to God and trust in his wisdom and power even when they lie far beyond his comprehension. In this regard, the purpose of the book of Ecclesiastes is strikingly similar to that of Job, although the approach is quite different.

The Disappointment of Earthly Pursuits

The author of Ecclesiastes spends a great deal of time describing his own efforts to find meaning in life by pursuing various earthly possibilities which seemed to offer promise. But in every case he found that all was vanity and a striving after wind.

1. *The vanity of human achievements.* As far as man can tell, achievements of former generations are soon for-

gotten and lose any significance they once may have had, and "new" achievements are ultimately meaningless because they are but repetitions of achievements of former generations (1:3-11).

"What has been is what will be,
and what has been done is what will be done;
and there is nothing new under the sun.
Is there a thing of which it is said,
'See, this is new'?
It has been already,
in the ages before us.
There is no remembrance of former things,
nor will there be any remembrance
of later things yet to happen
among those who come after" (1:9-11).

2. *The vanity of worldly wisdom.* "The Preacher" had pursued wisdom and knowledge as the solution to man's search for meaning and satisfaction. But the more he learned, the more he realized the perplexities of life, and he was more dissatisfied than ever (1:12-18). While "wisdom excels folly as light excels darkness" (2:13; see 7:4-6, 11-12, 19, 23-25; 10:2-3, 12-15), in reality the wise man knows very little of all there is to know (8:16-17), and he soon dies just like the fool and both are soon forgotten (2:13-17). This may be illustrated by a simple story.

"I have also seen this example of wisdom under the sun, and it seemed great to me. There was a little city with few men in it; and a great king came against it and besieged it, building great siegeworks against it. But there was found in it a poor wise man, and he by his wisdom delivered the city. Yet no one remembered that poor man. But I say that wisdom is better than might, though the poor man's wisdom is despised, and his words are not heeded" (9:13-16).

3. *The vanity of worldly pleasures.* The author had given himself to worldly pleasure: he had decided the key to life was to enjoy himself, to laugh a great deal,

and to drink wine. But he soon tired of this and realized how futile it was (2:1-3).

4. *The vanity of wealth.* In his search for real meaning in life, the writer turned to riches and culture. He built houses, planted vineyards, gardens, and parks and irrigated them, had many slaves or servants, amassed herds and flocks, silver and gold, and gathered to himself men and women singers for enjoyment and entertainment. But still he was not really satisfied (2:4-11).

"He who loves money will not be satisfied with money; nor he who loves wealth, with gain: this also is vanity. When goods increase, they increased who eat them; and what gain has their owner but to see them with his eyes?" (5:10-11).

When one dies, he must leave all his wealth to someone else, so that all the time and energy he exerted in amassing his fortunes are wasted (5:13-17). Furthermore, even in this life one often spends many years gaining wealth only to lose it to someone else (6:1-6).

5. *The vanity of hard work.* The author had also given himself to toil. But suddenly he realized that the blessings and benefits of his hard work would be given to others and enjoyed by them. Again he concludes that all is vanity (2:18-23; 4:7-8).

6. *The vanity of a mere external show of religion.* The author of Ecclesiastes also realized that mere external religious acts would not satisfy man's deepest longings. The sacrifice of fools is not acceptable to God; he does not desire or heed long and wordy prayers; and promises to pay vows are meaningless until the vows are paid (5:1-6).

Human helplessness over against the realities of life

"The Preacher" calls attention to many situations in life which are seemingly incongruous and over which man has no control. They seem to be unjust or over-whelming to man, but he can do nothing to change the way things are.

1. *Prosperity of the wicked and suffering of the righteous.* As in the book of Job, the author of Ecclesiastes calls attention to the apparent injustice of the wicked prospering and the righteous suffering, without any apparent redressing of the situation (3:16-4:41; 5:8-9; 7:15; 8:14; 10:5-7).

2. *Ingratitude for leadership and service.* At first, people are enthusiastic and supportive of a new ruler. But they soon tire of him and are ready for another, whom in turn they will quickly forget (4:13-16).

3. *Man's inability to know what is best or to control the future.* Life is too short and too complicated for one to know what is best for him. He is certainly in no position to question God's plans for man, for they are far beyond his comprehension and he cannot know what the future holds or control it (3:22; 6:10-12; 8:6-7, 17; 9:11-12; 10:14).

4. *The universal certainty of death.* All men, righteous and wicked, wise and foolish, rich and poor, will die, and there is no way to prevent this (2:14; 8:8; 9:1-6). The famous passage in 12:1-8 gives a very vivid description of aging and death in beautiful figurative language.

Victorious Living

Everything said in the last two sections might lead one to believe that for "The Preacher" life was tasteless, meaningless, empty, and futile. But all the things pointed out here are viewed totally from a human perspective. And the writer's purpose is to demonstrate powerfully and dramatically that if all there is to life is what man can see and experience on earth, "all is vanity." There-fore, man's only logical alternative is to live life in daily relationship to the living God. To be specific, the author commends a number of components which constitute victorious living.

1. *Fear God.* As elsewhere in the Wisdom Literature, the center of life in Ecclesiastes is to "fear God," that is, hold him in the highest respect, stand in awe of him, honor him (see Lesson II).

> "The end of the matter; all has been heard. Fear God, and keep his commandments; for this is the whole duty of man" (12:13).

> "Though a sinner does evil a hundred times and prolongs his life, yet I know that it will be well with those who fear God, because they fear before him; but it will be not be well with the wicked, neither will he prolong his days like a shadow, because he does not fear before God" (8:12-13; see further 5:7; 7:18).

2. *Trust God's Wisdom.* In spite of the seeming incongruities of life, accept by faith that God is in control and knows what is best.

> "Consider the work of God;
> who can make straight what he has made crooked?
> In the day of prosperity be joyful, and in the day of adversity consider; God has made the one as well as the other, so that man may not find out anything that will be after him" (7:13-14; see also 3:17; 12:14).

3. *Enjoy life.* Receive all God's gifts with gratitude, and enjoy all the aspects of life to the full. Certainly this does not mean to indulge oneself. Rather, the idea is that one is to receive God's gifts with thanksgiving and use them as God intended. This theme is very prominent in Ecclesiastes.

> "There is nothing better for a man than that he should eat and drink, and find enjoyment in his toil. This also, I saw, is from the hand of God; for apart from him who can eat or who can have enjoyment?"
> (2:24-25).

"I know that there is nothing better for them than to be happy and enjoy themselves as long as they live; also that it is God's gift to man that every one should eat and drink and take pleasure in all his toil" (3:12-13).

"Enjoy life with the wife whom you love, all the days of your vain life which he has given you under the sun, because that is your portion in life and in your toil at which you toil under the sun. Whatever your hand finds to do, do it with your might; for there is no work or thought or knowledge or wisdom in Sheol, to which you are going" (9:9-10; see in addition 3:22; 5:18-6:2; 8:15; 11:8-9).

4. *Be in subjection to rulers.* This is necessary in order that peace might prevail in society, and the different individuals in the community might have ample opportunity to grow and contribute their part to the good of the whole (8:2-5; 10:20).

5. *Be slow to criticize.* It is easy to see the sins of others, but more often than not he who criticizes those sins is guilty of the same.

"Do not give heed to all the things that men say, lest you hear your servant cursing you; your heart knows that many times you have yourself cursed others" (7:21-22).

6. *Be aware you are a sinner.* Like the rest of the Bible, the book of Ecclesiastes teaches that all men are sinners.

"Surely there is not a righteous man on earth who does good and never sins" (7:20).

7. *Do not be excessive in righteousness or wickedness.* God can work with a balanced person, but an extremist is not dependable.

"Be not righteous overmuch, and do not make yourself overwise; why should you destroy yourself? Be not wicked overmuch, neither be a fool; why should you die before your time?" (7:16-17).

8. *Be willing to take a risk.* Since the future is uncertain from a purely human perspective, and since God is in control of everything, one must not hesitate to venture out, trusting God to bless the godly man's efforts with prosperity.

"Cast your bread upon the waters,
for you will find it after many days . . .
If the clouds are full of rain,
they empty themselves on the earth . . .
He who observes the wind will not sow;
and he who regards the clouds will not reap . . .
In the morning sow your seed, and at evening withhold not your hand; for you do not know which will prosper, this or that, or whether both alike will be good" (11:1, 3, 4, 6 — read all of verses 1-6).

The context shows that this paragraph is (not) talking about benevolence (contrary to what some have thought), but about taking a risk or venturing out in various types of undertakings. Verse 1, for example, probably has in mind maritime commerce.

9. *Live a godly life.* Since life is short and death certain, the most important thing for one who fears God to do each day is to live a godly life. The writer of Ecclesiastes specifies a number of things which are included in this. (a) Do not oppress the poor or take a bribe (7:7). (b) Be slow to anger (7:9). (c) Avoid the harlot or prostitute (7:26). (d) Establish a good reputation (7:1). (e) Put God first in your youth while you are still healthy and strong (11:9; 12:1).

Review   Questions

1. Give five views as to the perspective of the author of Ecclesiastes. Discuss the arguments for and against each view. Which view do you think is preferable? Why?

2. Name four ways the book of Ecclesiastes has been analyzed. Discuss each of these. Which do you think is correct? Support your view with good arguments.   *p 128*

3. From a purely human point of view, everything in life is vanity. List the six things pointed out in this lesson which the author of Ecclesiastes declares to be vanity. Ecclesiastes 1:3-11, 12-18; 2:1-3, 4-11, 18-23; 5:1-6. Discuss each of these.   *p 128-130*

4. According to Ecclesiastes, what are four things in life which appear to be incongruous and over which man has no control? Ecclesiastes 5:8-9; 4:13-16; 6:10-12; 9:1-6. Discuss each of these.   *p 131*

5. What is the ultimate purpose of the writer of Ecclesiastes in emphasizing the vanity of all earthly pursuits and the incongruities of life over which man has no control? Discuss.

6. Enumerate nine positive things proclaimed by the author of Ecclesiastes which constitute victorious living. Ecclesiastes 12:13; 7:13-14; 2:24-25; 8:2-5; 7:21-22, 20, 16-17; 11:1-6; 7:7, 9, 26, 1; 11:9; 12:1. Discuss the practical value of each of these for daily godly living.   *p 132-34*

Bibliography

Numerous enclyclopedia articles, books, journal articles, and commentaries have been written on the books of Job, Proverbs, Ecclesiastes, and Song of Solomon, as well as on the Wisdom Literature of the Old Testament and of the ancient Near East, and the Old Testament Apocryphal wisdom books. Here only a very few publications in English are mentioned, each of which may be consulted for much more extensive bibliographical references in several modern languages.

Bible Enclyclopedias

Articles on Wisdom Literature and each of the Old Testament wisdom books in each of the following.

The International Standard Bible Encyclopedia — Fully Revised

The Interpreter's Dictionary of the Bible, 4 volumes, plus the Supplementary Volume.

McKenzie, John L., S. J., *Dictionary of the Bible.*

Wycliffe Bible Encyclopedia, 2 volumes.

Works on Wisdom Literature

Crenshaw, James L. *Old Testament Wisdom: An Introduction.* Atlanta: John Knox Press, 1981.

Murphy, Roland E. *Wisdom Literature of the Old Testament.* Grand Rapids, Mich.: Wm. B. Eerdmans Publishing Co., 1981.

Rankin, O.S. *Israel's Wisdom Literature.* Edinburgh: T & T Clark, 1936.

Scott, R. B. Y. *The Way of Wisdom in the Old Testament.* New York: Macmillan, 1971.

Commentaries and Special Studies

The following sets of commentaries may be used with benefit.

The Anchor Bible

The Cambridge Bible for Schools and Colleges

The International Critical Commentary

The Interpreter's Bible
The Interpreter's One-Volume Commentary on the Bible
The Jerome Biblical Commentary
The New Century Bible Commentary
The New International Commentary on the Old Testament
The Old Testament Library
Peake's Commentary on the Bible
Torch Bible Commentaries
Tyndale Old Testament Commentaries
The following special studies are helpful.

Gammie, John, editor. *Israelite Wisdom: Theological and Literary Essays in Honor of Samel Terrien.* Missoula, Montana: Scholars Press, 1978.

Gordis, Robert. *The Book of Job.* New York: The Jewish Theological Seminary of America, 1978.

Gordis, Robert. *Koheleth: The Man and His World.* New York: Schocken, 1951.

Lambert, W. G. *Babylonian Wisdom Literature.* Oxford: At the Clarendon Press, 1960.

McKane, W. *Prophets and Wise Men.* London: SCM Press, 1965.

Pritchard, James B. *Ancient Near Eastern Texts relating to the Old Testament.* Third Edition, with supplement. Princeton: University Press, 1969.

von Rad, Gerhard, *Wisdom in Israel.* Nashville: Abingdon Press, 1972.

Journal Articles

Barr, James, "The Book of Job and Its Modern Interpreters," *Bulletin of the John Rylands Library,* vol. 54 (1971), pp. 28-46.

Holm-Nielsen, S. "The Book of Ecclesiastes and the Interpretations of it in Jewish and Christian Theology," *Annual of the Swedish Theological Institute,* vol. 10 (1975-76), pp. 38-96.

Priest, John F. "Where is Wisdom to be Placed?" *Journal of Bible and Religion,* vol. 31 (1963), pp. 275-282.

Scott, R. B. Y. "The Study of Wisdom Literature," *Interpretation,* vol. 24 (1970), pp. 20-45.